T0373015

Good Night, I Love You

Good Night, I Love You

A WIDOW'S AWAKENING
from PAIN *to* PURPOSE

Jené Ray Barranco

New York   Nashville

FaithWords
Hachette Book Group
1290 Avenue of the Americas, New York, NY 10104
faithwords.com
twitter.com/faithwords

First Edition: September 2017

FaithWords is a division of Hachette Book Group, Inc. The FaithWords name
and logo are trademarks of Hachette Book Group, Inc.

The publisher is not responsible for websites (or their content) that are not
owned by the publisher.

The Hachette Speakers Bureau provides a wide range of authors for speaking events.
To find out more, go to www.hachettespeakersbureau.com or call (866) 376-6591.

Additional copyright information is on page 228.

Library of Congress Cataloging-in-Publication Data
Names: Barranco, Jené Ray, author.
Title: Good night, I love you : a widow's awakening from pain to purpose /
Jené Ray Barranco.
Description: first [edition]. | New York : Faith Words, 2017.
Identifiers: LCCN 2017016496 | ISBN 9781455598441 (hardcover) | ISBN
9781455598434 (ebook)
Subjects: LCSH: Barranco, Jené Ray. | Spouses—Death—Psychological aspects.
| Bereavement—Religious aspects—Christianity. | Consolation. | Widows—
Religious life.
Classification: LCC BV4908 .B375 2017 | DDC 248.8/66092 [B] —dc23
LC record available at https://lccn.loc.gov/2017016496

ISBNs: 978-1-4555-9844-1 (hardcover), 978-1-4555-9843-4 (ebook)

Printed in the United States of America
LSC-C

10 9 8 7 6 5 4 3 2 1

For Mia, Julia, and Michael Anthony,
my brave warriors beside me on this
unchartered path.
Your fortitude inspires me.

And for my Michael:
son, brother, husband, father, architect, singer,
writer, worshipper, friend.
You did them all well.

Contents

"I'm Michael"

Sᴇᴘᴛᴇᴍʙᴇʀ 5, 1986. Cʀᴀɪɢ, ᴍʏ ᴏʟᴅᴇʀ ʙʀᴏᴛʜᴇʀ, asked me to join him at Poets, a popular piano bar in Jackson, Mississippi. On the weekends, it was *the* place to go for the twenty- and thirty-something crowd. And actually, the forty- and fifty-something crowd as well, but they sat on the "other" side of the room on the red leather stools by the long wooden bar. The smoky mirror behind the bartenders revealed the revelry in the place. I had never been there—apparently I was one of the few eligible single women my age who had not. Craig took me there because, as he said, "You've got to hear this guy who can sing 'Sittin' on the Dock of the Bay' like nobody's business! Even better than Otis Redding himself!"

I soon found out that "this guy," an up-and-coming young architect by day and an equally talented R&B singer by night, was the most sought after bachelor in northeast Jackson and knew almost everyone in town. But I had never heard of him, and he had never heard of me.

At the last minute, my mom snapped a quick picture of Craig

and me before we walked out the door. I was looking very eighties in my red, black, and white color-blocked cotton sweater, black pencil skirt, red short pumps, colored plastic earrings, and of course, the ever-popular four-inch-high bangs and too much eye makeup. Where were the fashion police in the eighties?

As we walked into Poets on the upper level, we saw This Guy behind the red wooden piano bar, standing tall above the crowd, crooning into the microphone with his eyes tightly shut. He was built like a linebacker, had long, naturally curly black hair, and wore an artsy pair of thin wire-rimmed glasses. Behind him stood a wall of stained glass and the members of the Andy Hardwick Trio, three exceptionally talented African American musicians accompanied by this handsome, Caucasian football player singing into the microphone as if he were in his own little world. I remember thinking how soulful he appeared while he sang with his eyes closed, holding the microphone tightly against his chin. He seemed oblivious to the crowd, which was elbow-to-elbow people talking and determined to see and be seen.

Not long after we arrived, the band took a break, and This Guy began making his way through the crowd. As he approached us, he said to Craig, "Hey, how you doing?"

It turned out they recognized one another from the Courthouse Racquet Club, where Craig was a manager and tennis pro. This Guy lifted weights there, but they had never actually met. So Craig introduced himself and then me.

This Guy turned to me and, while leaning in so that I could hear him, said, *"I'm Michael,"* in the most peaceful and soothing voice I had ever heard come out of a man's mouth.

"I'm Jené," I said as I leaned toward his ear and added that I also worked at the racquet club, at the front desk. I was accustomed to repeating my name because many people have never heard it before, and that night was no different. He asked me to repeat it, which I did, then he said it for clarification. I had never heard my name pronounced so beautifully. (He even said the "J" with the correct French pronunciation.) It was as if the room fell quiet. The two of us, and the moment, seemed to be surrounded by a wall from another realm.

The band break was quickly over, and Michael made his way back to the microphone. After a few more songs, Craig and I decided to call it a night. As I stood on the upper level near the front door, I turned, looking Michael's way for one last glance. In a rare moment, he happened to have his eyes open and made eye contact with me while he was singing. He nodded with a smile, and I walked out the door.

For some reason, I wasn't surprised when he walked through the double glass doors of the racquet club the next morning. He was wearing a loose-fitting T-shirt that was cut into a tank top, which revealed that he truly was built like a linebacker. We talked for a moment about the previous evening at Poets, and then he went out to the pool. He was there not to exercise but to lie in the sun and catch up on his trade magazines—I saw a couple of *Architectural Digests* peeking out of the top of his leather satchel. But soon enough, he came back to the front desk for some juice, which he put on his tab. Then he kept coming back for more juice, and more juice, and more juice. Each time we talked a little more, a little more, and a little more. His voice sounded so peaceful and calm even though his mouth seemed stuck in a grin.

He "forgot" to close his tab.

After Michael left the club, I called my mom to tell her that I would not be coming straight home from work that night. I told her about my conversations with Michael and this feeling I had that he would come back and ask me out for dinner.

I was right.

He showed up right before closing and told me how terrible he felt for not paying earlier and that he wanted to settle up with me. He paid for the juice and chatted with me as I finished closing out the register. He walked with me outside and asked if I wanted to go grab a bite somewhere.

We went to McB's, a very casual and popular dive near the Ross Barnett Reservoir, Jackson's man-made lake. The reservoir had become a water-sport and fishing attraction. Customers could walk inside McB's with wet hair, swimsuit cover-ups, cut-off shorts, and flip-flops after having spent the day water-skiing or fishing. We found a table in this log cabin–style joint and ordered some shrimp po' boys and cold beer. We spent hours that night talking about our faith in God, our large families, our dreams, and even our mutual desire for children (not necessarily together, but just our personal dreams for them). Two weeks later we professed our love to one another, and four months later, on Christmas Eve, we were engaged. We married on September 5, 1987—exactly one year after we met.

The picture my mom snapped of Craig and me before going to Poets that fate-driven night came to represent the beginning of a beautiful, extraordinary journey that I never could have anticipated. About twenty years after we were married, I made copies of the picture, put them into frames, and gave one to Michael and one to my brother. Craig took pride in knowing he was responsible for bringing us together that singular night. Michael never let me get rid of that color-blocked sweater. It stayed in a box of wedding memorabilia our entire marriage. To him, it represented a magical moment—when I walked into his life as I walked into Poets that early September evening in 1986.

After much prayer, we began trying to start a family. Exactly five years after we married, our first child, Mia, entered this world with all of her sweetness, flexibility, empathetic heart, and melancholy spirit. Four years later, Julia arrived and immediately showed her insatiable appetite for living and learning. In spite of her bold and confident spirit, she was never one to be too far away from either Michael or me. (Her nickname later became Velcro Girl because at times she sticks to your side.) Miraculously, just twenty months later, Michael Anthony came onto the scene. A spirit of adventure and curiosity showed itself at an early age. He thrived on one-on-one time with Michael or me as well as with one of his sisters, social time with friends, and physical activity, always with a tender heart.

During those early years while the children were very young, I developed the habit of rising while it was still dark to pray and read my Bible. My days took every ounce of strength out of me. I rose each morning desperate to sit at God's feet to receive more strength. I had an insatiable hunger to understand His will and purpose for my life within the larger story He was writing for me.

I woke at four thirty in the morning for an hour and a half of focused time with God, then spent the rest of the early morning hours writing until the first peep from the children rang out into the meditative silence; a day in the life with small children began all over again. For several years, all I read was the book of Proverbs. With the wisdom of Proverbs as ammunition for my daily battles, a miraculous measure of peace surrounded me during those physically taxing years, and in the years to come. Proverbs 4:25 and 26 became my daily mantra: "Let your eyes look straight ahead, and your eyelids look right before you. Ponder the path of your feet, and let all your ways be established" (NKJV). These words kept me grounded and focused as a young mother. I had no idea how crucial this verse would become for my very survival through life's most difficult times.

While Mia was still a toddler, Michael and I prayerfully chose to be a homeschooling family. We saw our homeschooling lifestyle as a stunningly romantic way to experience and celebrate life, education, and family as a consummate whole. The heartbeat of our family flourished in our french country kitchen. Countless meals and conversations nurtured us around the old wooden breakfast table I'd found at a garage sale the year Mia was born.

From breakfasts with buckwheat pancakes or streusel muffins, to homemade soups or sandwiches made with fresh bread for lunch, to our gatherings at dinner for grilled salmon, risotto, or lamb ragout over polenta, the aroma of a full life was savored in our home. Our family days were full of life, loving, learning, forgiving, sharing, and feasting.

Michael and I lived in our own little universe full of stolen glances, love notes, dates, gifts, private moments, whispers of sweet words that only the two of us could hear—and the private affair we shared with our Heavenly Father. I thought our days would continue to look like this into the future, as we grew old together. But seasons change.

Our fairy-tale family lasted for twenty-four years. Then, on February 22, 2011, life as we knew it was wiped out, as if by a tsunami, in one devastating instant.

I lost the love of my life, Michael Anthony Barranco, Sr., in a car wreck. He had driven out of town for an overnight business trip, to be away for only twenty-four hours.

Our last Valentine's Day fell just eight days before the accident.

The kids ate together, and then Michael and I ordered takeout and watched a movie in the den. We told them it was our date night and they were to stay upstairs. Michael let me choose the movie and even gave me the green light for any romantic comedy I wanted. I chose *Something's Gotta Give*. We had seen it several times, but it's always worth seeing again. That night we laughed harder than we had ever laughed. The kids later said, "We heard Dad laughing all the way upstairs!"

Diane Keaton's role as the lead female is a playwright. One of our favorite lines was actually just a spoken thought about the conversation she's having with her love interest, played by

Jack Nicholson. She stops in the middle of what she's doing and says, more to herself than to him, "Did one of us just say something interesting?" Michael and I frequently tried to catch ourselves saying "something interesting" that would be good movie dialogue.

While we lay in bed together about a month before Michael died, he stayed completely still for a moment, then whispered to me, "Is that someone coming up the stairs"—a short pause—"or is that my heart beating?" He paused again, and then we both laughed and he said, "That would be a great line in a movie!"

What was most amazing about our last Valentine's Day was that he stayed awake through the entire movie. He always fell asleep during movies at home and even sometimes at the theater. It was because he had stopped moving, thinking, and creating. Both he and Michael Anthony had two gears: on or off, awake or asleep, full throttle or in park. Michael Anthony has been like that since he was old enough to walk. We laughed while watching him fall asleep. Even now our son asks a few questions and yawns in a loud, sighing way, and then he's asleep. Like father, like son.

That last Valentine's Day, Michael decided to spread the gifts out one by one, something he had never done before. The first gift was a beautiful gardening book for us to look through together as inspiration for our garden. We liked discussing the details of the garden. We dreamed, got dirty, and sweated together in the garden. After watching the movie, he gave me a little framed piece of embroidery that read, "Any time, any place, any where...I will be there for you." On the day I found out about the accident, I discovered that it was still sitting in the den, where I had opened it. What a precious gift. What a thoughtful man—a simple, small, yet huge gift.

The final gift came that night right as we were drifting off to sleep. He said, "I also paid for you to have a ninety-minute massage with Marion. You need that. Be sure and do that soon for yourself." Without my mate, I was bereft of physical touch; with this gift, Michael unknowingly met my needs ahead of time.

When all of Michael's things from his car were brought back to me the night of the accident, I noticed that he had slipped the Valentine's card I had just given him into the outside pocket of his computer case. He usually carried my most recent card around with him. He pulled it out and read it over and over when he needed a momentary retreat from the daily grind. It transported him to the safety, peace, and love of the children, our home, and me.

The outside of my card read, "Together," and on the inside I had written, "forever. Happy Valentine's Day to my husband, the love of my life."

His card to me read, "I want to hold your hand," and inside he had added, "and talk less, listen more, hold you, know you like never before, learn with you, laugh with you, cry with you, pray with you, be with you and love you."

I never opened the gardening book. I completely lost my gardening mojo after he died. It took me three years to begin to inch my way back into the dirt, and then I was able to begin with only a container garden. The embroidery sits on a stone shelf above the fireplace in my writing room. It took me several months after he died to get around to the massage. I cried silently through every minute of it.

CHAPTER 2

Tsunami

Three things amaze me, no, four things I'll never
understand—how an eagle flies so high in the sky . . .

—PROVERBS 30:18–19A (MSG)

THE AIR IS PARALYZED. Had a pine needle drifted to the ground
from one of the towering trees surrounding us, I believe I could
have heard it. There is a large crowd, but they are silent around
us. Beyond the pond and trees I can see one of the commercial
developments Michael designed. It seemed right to bury him
near nature and architectural design. The preacher speaks the final words. No one stirs. A deafening stillness hangs in the air like
the silence between a flash of lightning and a crash of thunder.
It is finished—the tsunami that struck only days before when I
learned of Michael's death is suddenly calm for the moment. I
sit in my chair under the tent facing Michael's casket while holding an eagle feather in my hand. I feel the silence crushing all of
us. The reality of Michael's permanent absence falls over me like
a lead blanket. I am suffocating.

I sit with our children in the front row, the four of us finger-
ing our eagle feathers as if we are touching his heart one last
time.

Michael had been a member of the Order of the Arrow as a
Boy Scout and competed in Indian dance competitions wearing costumes he sewed and beaded by hand. He romanced the
notion that he should have been born a Native American. Like
the American Indians, Michael held a reverence for the bald eagle. As destiny would have it, he came upon the carcass of a
bald eagle while walking in the woods of northeast Mississippi
about a year before his death. He received official permission
to keep the feathers and placed them in a special box.

Native Americans were given an eagle feather for extreme
acts of valor—an earned mark of distinction. Because the eagle
flies closer to the Creator than any other bird, they believed
eagles were messengers of God, as they are able to see the
flow of change below. They see the big picture and can alert
us about what is to come so that we may respond or prepare.
Receiving an eagle feather is, then, a symbol from above, and
they can only be earned one at a time. Was Michael's discovery
of an eagle's carcass with all its feathers, instead of just one, a
sign that he had attained a lifetime's worth of valor? Or was it
even a possible alert regarding what lay ahead for us?

According to Native American wisdom, an eagle feather
must never touch the ground unless it is buried with a fallen
warrior. I wanted to honor my fallen warrior. I allowed the
children to choose a feather from his collection to bury with
their father.

It is time to lay the eagle feathers on Michael's casket. The stagnant air continues to choke any sound. The birds are silent. No one moves a muscle. After a long, smothering pause, I will my body out of the chair and my children follow my lead, each one of us holding an eagle feather. I usher them toward the casket, then step aside, signaling them to go before me. One at a time, I watch them gingerly approach, then lay the feather to rest on top of the casket. *Where does this courage come from? This strength to even stand?* I wonder as I observe this moment. My own pain shifts to overwhelming compassion for my children. What I would do to protect their hearts! Oh, dear Jesus, catch their bleeding hearts! Can you see them, God? Are they going to make it? Will you protect them? As I watch each of them, my heart grows heavier as it sinks deeper into my already caving chest. They are so young. They should not have to bury their father.

Michael Anthony steps forward looking solemn, glazed, and shell-shocked. As I look at my twelve-year-old son in his Boy Scout uniform, I am overcome. He's lost his Bud. His best friend. His mentor. The only man in his life. His compass to manhood. Oh, God! How can I raise this young boy to become all that he is meant to be? How can I possibly meet his needs?

Julia, now fourteen years old, moves forward. I notice she is already taking on her own private way of carrying the pain. Crying hard, but controlling the sobs by lifting her shoulders and holding her breath, she goes through the motions despite her fear and uncertainty. Lord, calm the storm for her. Bring some semblance of order back to her life. Protect her passion for life. Bring her to safety. Hold her, God! Rescue her!

I notice again how suffocating the air feels. My ears are ringing. How is it so quiet outside? I glance off into the distance beyond the casket for a deep breath and catch sight of a photographer with a zoom lens aimed at us. The only things I hear in the vacuum of silence are our footsteps on the green indoor-outdoor carpet.

Mia takes her turn. The word *angel* enters my mind. At seventeen she is the oldest, but her age does not give her any more understanding or any less pain than her younger brother and sister. The heart of an angel—God, will this change? Can you keep her heart as tender as it always has been? Her dad affirmed her, affirmed her goodness, every day. Will you do that for her, God? Give her hope! Don't let this pain build a wall around her tender heart!

I want to reach out and pull them in to me as if that will protect them from any future harm, but I know it won't. Protecting them from this pain is not possible. Pain is inevitable. They step slightly aside. We are now tightly clustered together near the casket, drawing on the strength from standing together as one. I feel their presence behind me as I take my small step to the casket. I feel exposed, abandoned, vulnerable, and alone in a cold world. I place my feather next to the others, then place one hand flat on the top of the casket. I don't want to say good-bye. If I stand here long enough, maybe I can somehow prolong my connection with Michael on this earth. My feet are stuck. I take deep breaths, trying to maintain some kind of composure, but crashing waves of grief hit me in the gut and take my breath away. Tears overtake me. I place my other hand on top of the casket for support. My cries turn into wails from the pit of my stomach as I fall onto the casket. I cannot tear myself away from this place. No one moves or breathes. A reverenced silence hovers in the air with only my cries filling the void.

In the midst of my tears, I hear the voice of my close friend Kevin Cooley trying to speak. He stands at the other end of the casket. And finally his words break through my cries, his voice radiating peaceful compassion:

Unless a grain of wheat falls into the ground and dies, it remains alone. But if it dies, it produces much grain. Today we are not burying our dead; we are planting our seed...you are planting your seed. Harvest will come. Because this life is not all there is or all there will ever be. It's not over. We are eternal and we shall meet again...and it won't always hurt this bad.

I take a deep breath. Still, not a soul moves. Another moment of silence, then Michael's brother, Vince, a professional musician, steps up to the casket, holding a piece of paper with a song he has written.

Rejoice...
So you don't have to worry any more
We must rejoice in what has come to be
For he has claimed an early, just reward
It's all he ever wanted us to see

Finally, the release comes. I move away from the casket, and I sense that everyone is breathing again.

Later when someone asks me about the graveside service, I cannot even recall the preacher who spoke. In truth, I barely remember the beginning days. The barrage of visitors, house-guests, and meetings kept me breathing. Conversations and meetings were a blur. My body and mind were numb. My friend Adrienne, who lives in Mobile, Alabama, came to stay with me for a few days to help run my household. Months later, during a conversation with her, she pointed out I had completely forgotten her time at my house. Once she reminded me, it all came back, but until then the memory had vanished.

A couple of months after the funeral I take the kids to Rosemary Beach, Florida, where we always went as a family. It is our first time to go away as a new family unit of four—instead of five. As I drive back to the beach house one afternoon, a "reality check" strikes my heart. Is he really gone from this world? How is that possible? He was just here! We just had lunch with him at this place. We ate at that table right there. He bought me a purse in this store. We tried on clothes here every year. We have driven this stretch a hundred times together. Weren't we just here with him?

Back home in Jackson, it's the same.

How could he really be gone? Didn't he just plant those flowers in our garden? We just had a family dinner together. We just roasted marshmallows together on the back patio. I just helped him organize his office for this year, and we were not finished. He just bought a bunch of nice work clothes that he had not even worn yet. He just took Michael Anthony

GOOD NIGHT, I LOVE YOU

camping. We just had a glass of wine together. He just kissed me good-bye. We just talked on the phone. He just got a new haircut. He just bought his new car. Wasn't our summer vacation just yesterday? Didn't we just order takeout and watch a movie on the couch together? Where did he go?

He *really* isn't coming back.

This *is* real. He *really* is in heaven now, and we *really* miss him.

The children and I make great efforts to accept the reality and move forward each and every moment. I believe we're able to do so only because of the prayers of so many people and because God's grace is tangible daily. It is as if we are newborn birds in a nest, desperately looking up to our Heavenly Father for protection and our daily sustenance. We are entirely dependent on Him as each new day dawns without Michael.

Grief hits like a tsunami. It is a tidal wave of emotions, pain, and crashing waves that are utterly overwhelming. Following the initial devastation of a tsunami comes a series of crushing waves, the wave train. At first, a steady, continual crashing of emotional waves of grief crushed me daily, sometimes to the point of suffocation. I barely pulled my head above each wave in time to sustain the next onslaught. Then smaller waves from the wave train washed over me every day—as they still do today, every time I see the signs of his life that is no longer there.

Michael started a Boy Scout troop at our church as an outreach to the boys in the surrounding community. Many of the boys came from broken families and did not have a father figure or male influence of any kind in their lives. Michael saw Scouting as an opportunity to help these boys grow in their confidence, leadership, values, and life discipline. Michael Anthony was also in this troop, which gave him even more time to spend with his father.

It intrigues me that Michael started this troop to help lead young boys without a male influence, without a father figure in their lives—and then our son became one of them.

One of the things Michael taught his troop was the well-known Scout saying, "Leave No Trace." It means respect others and respect creation as a whole. We taught Michael Anthony how to practice this in our home. After watching a movie in the den, Leave No Trace. After changing his clothes, Leave No Trace. After creating something, Leave No Trace. After eating a snack, Leave No Trace. Since Michael's death, many people have told me, "You are going to see Michael everywhere you turn because he left so much of himself."

I see Michael in the garden where we worked and dreamed together. I see a trace of him in the kitchen that we designed together and where he moaned in delight when a flavor or an aroma moved him. I see a trace of him in the dining room sconces: after searching for months, he finally located the perfect ones in South Africa. I see his trace in the summer, when the fig trees, which he brought in from Atlanta, are producing the luscious fruit he thought was heavenly. I see a trace of him when I look at our garden fountain, which he gave me one Christmas and threw out his back trying to place in the garden, in the dark, on Christmas Eve. I see him when I look at my urban chicken coop from my kitchen window that he so creatively designed and built himself by adding on to our swing-set fort—just because I had always wanted chickens. Yes, he left a big trace of his goodness, his generosity, his beauty, and his thoughtfulness—traces of his heart for God, his hard work, and his preparedness.

But I also notice where he's left no trace.

There is no trace of his daily rhythms. The half-finished cup of black coffee, Italian roast, which he left in the same place on the kitchen counter every morning as he left for work—it is no longer there. The blanket and Bible that stayed on or next to his favorite leather chair, where he spent the early morning hours, is no longer there. His clothes for the dry cleaner that he would drape over a rod in our closet are no longer there. The smell of his cologne hanging in the morning air is no longer there. His frequent love notes that came via text messages are no longer there. His dirty exercise clothes that he dropped on the floor next to the laundry basket are no longer there. His empty wineglass that I washed by hand is no longer there. His brand-new Land Rover is no longer there. His voice saying "Babe, I'm gone. I love you...I'll call you later!" as he walked out the door each morning is no longer there. When I make my bed, his rumpled side is no longer there. These were all traces of life, which is no longer there. Every time I discover another trace of the absence of his life, another wave washes over me.

The most obvious place where no trace is left behind is next to me in bed. Julia quickly acquired Michael's pillow so she could smell him at night. It was not until about six weeks after he died that I slept by myself for the first time. My kids, my sister Julie, Michael's sister Lesa, and a couple other friends who came for extended stays took turns sleeping in bed with me so I wouldn't have to sleep alone. Once the overnight visitors stopped coming and went back to their own homes, their own states, or in my dear friend Nanette's case, even their own countries, my house seemed suddenly empty, and I felt alone all of the time, not just at night.

Nanette and I have been close friends for twenty-nine years; we are like sisters, really. We coached cheerleaders together, led cheer camps together, and bought our first houses next to each other. We took family vacations together and took turns having children every other year until there were six kids between us, all girls except for Michael Anthony coming in as the caboose. At the time of Michael's death, she and her husband, Peter, were living in Sydney, Australia. Peter and Michael had been close friends from the beginning as well. We were a foursome.

I had her with me for two weeks after Michael died. Her presence made me feel a small measure of safety. If visitors arrived, she sometimes acted as my own personal bouncer, all five feet and three inches of her. She explained to them that I needed rest and graciously answered all of their questions and spoke to them on my behalf. She had a notebook with running lists of people who stopped by, phone messages left, or questions that arose in her mind. She received the meals arriving daily and kept all the food organized in my refrigerator. But the biggest gifts she gave me were of her heart, her time, and her listening ears. She continuously watched my back with concern for my health and overall grief status. While most people focused on what they could do to help run my household, Nanette focused completely on my personal needs. She was able to do this simply because we had shared such a large portion of our life experience together. Because of her presence in my kids' lives from birth, she was able to step in and meet some of their emotional needs as well.

After Nanette spent two weeks with me, it came time for her to fly back home. The wave train struck again. The reality of being alone came crashing into my heart. I remember walking quietly and somberly up to my bedroom, alone, for the very first time. The air felt still. The house seemed particularly quiet. The weight of grief and loneliness pressed in a little harder against my chest.

In spite of my sporadic ability to sleep, that night my sleep was surprisingly sound, but then it came time to wake up—and realize Michael's side of the bed was empty.

This was a bittersweet moment. The bitterness for the obvious reasons. The sweetness was that I woke like that—by myself—most mornings, since Michael had been an early riser. He would be already in prayer, reading his Bible, exercising at River Hills, or walking the dog.

On the rare days I had awoken before him, mostly on Saturdays, I enjoyed turning my head to stare at him as he slept. Michael slept on his stomach but slightly pulled up on one side with one arm up over his head on the pillow and the other tucking in the corner of the pillow under his chin. I liked stretching my leg across our king-size bed to rub my foot on his or to feel his calf. Sometimes I placed my hand on his bicep. If his head was turned the other way, I liked looking at the wild nest of messy curls that had formed at his crown. If I got out of bed before him, I often leaned down and kissed him on his cheekbone. Most of the time he slept through it.

We both preferred praying out loud, and our morning routines allowed us to do so. My routine has changed. Since Michael's death I've been unable to speak to God apart from saying "Thank you" one night through my tears. It was all I could do to thank God that I was still alive and had made it through another day.

That first morning I am alone, after Nanette leaves, I wake up and lie still in the silence. I hadn't realized until this moment how comforting it had been to hear my husband's morning sounds from downstairs. After I picture him and listen to my memory of sounds, I begin trying to pray aloud, but I suddenly realize I need to change my prayer habits.

My prayers always followed a pattern: thankfulness, acknowledgment of His power and presence in my life, praying God's will, welcoming His kingdom's power, and forgiveness. Next, my prayers always turned to Michael. Years ago, a female teacher at our church had said to all of the women present, "If we aren't lifting our husbands up in prayer and surrounding them with prayer, who will?" That comment shook me. Since that day, I prayed for Michael every day. Sometimes he even got a double dose of prayer; if there was something special going on I'd pray for him throughout the day.

I try to start down "my Michael path of prayer." I feel lost. I can't find words—or even my desire to pray. A couple of painfully silent minutes pass. I redirect my path. I think about praying for Michael's architectural firm, but God's presence suddenly overcomes me. I stop speaking. In a moment,

I feel the comfort and realization that my prayers for Michael through all of our years together had been answered. I am now speechless. As God promised in the book of Psalms, He *had* stood up on His holy hill and heard my prayers, and came to Michael's rescue every day of his life. The magnitude of this truth brings me to my knees.

Morning time has always been my favorite time of day. I enjoy the way life eases back into being. But since Michael died, morning is the hardest part of my day. I cry more, remember more, and seem to need him more. This is why I choose to write in the morning hours. It engages my mind and directs my thoughts and emotions onto something specific. I want to focus on every aspect of our lives together and write it all down while the memories are fresh. I need to pour out my pain in an effort to lighten the weight my body now seems to carry at all times. I'm thankful for my alone time with Michael's memory and my hours of grieving in the early mornings. I miss him beyond words, and this first morning alone brings about a deafening void. I meditate on this verse: "I rise before the dawning of the morning, and cry for help; I hope in Your word. My eyes are awake through the night watches, that I may meditate on Your word" (Ps. 119:147–148 NKJV).

I begin waking up between two and four in the morning every day, alone, heart racing, stomach on fire. These panic attacks are always worse in the dark hours of the early morning. I still cannot find words for prayers in these moments. Release comes only when I bolt out of bed to my computer to "give birth" to my thoughts. Writing helps the physical symptoms subside momentarily. In the past, the only times I had ever awakened in the middle of the night, outside of for crying children, were when I needed to pray, listen to God, or write. If my reason for bolting out of bed had to do with writing, it was always something God inspired.

During one of these God-inspired pre-dawn writing sessions, my thoughts turn toward the whole concept of "the body of Christ"—not only what it means, but also what it looks like. Galatians 6:2 says, "Carry each other's burdens, and in this way you will fulfill the law of Christ" (NIV). The trick is in *knowing* each other's burdens, which is not easy even in the most intimate relationships. We live in a prideful society that communicates the ideas "I am fine . . . I can do it myself . . . I don't want to concern you with my problems; everyone has enough problems of their own."

This kind of thinking is a lie. I know I am not the only one who wants people to think I don't have burdens and all is well. If we weren't going to have burdens, why would God command us to carry them for each other? I've always been a very private person, not so much keeping my burdens to myself as simply private in general. Michael and I were at peace, and happiest, in the presence of our family, within our "four walls," the garden being included within those walls. Life was rich in that place. It's different now. I have needs that can be met only by those outside the walls. I need to have other people, the body of Christ, help carry some of these burdens as much as *they* have a need to carry them. The only way this can happen is if I am gut-wrenchingly honest, filleted open for all to see the injury.

Expose the wound, share the burden—this is how healing can begin.

Steve, our assistant minister, comes over to talk one morning and describes to me how the body of Christ works together as a community during times of tragedy and pain. The author Philip Yancey calls it *connective tissue*. When we have a cut in our physical bodies, it hurts most where the injury occurred. In this case, my heart and the hearts of my children and our extended families are the points of injury, but the connective tissue around the wound, the body of Christ, is tender and hurting as well. The closer you get to the point of injury, the greater the pain, but the whole area, including the connective tissue, hurts.

I'm stirred as I recognize how this truth plays out in my life during these early times of excruciating pain. I am bleeding profusely. I've lost much blood from the wound. The pain and the wound are raw. The pain is real—more than I could ever have imagined. I don't want to hide any of my pain, my burdens. What would I gain by hiding them? Hiding our burdens only makes them heavier.

This has been the hardest path in life I have ever journeyed. It has been frightfully cold and lonely. I've grappled in the dark for what already seems like a lifetime. I miss my husband with all of my soul. If I could just smell his skin and touch his hair. At times I can barely breathe without reminding myself to inhale and exhale. The air is always heavy. My vision is blurred. Sometimes I can't even think. What might appear to be baby steps each day are not small at all. My heart thanks God for the body of Christ, the community of believers who surround me like the connective tissue in my body. They hurt with me and for me. They instinctively hold me, some only in their prayers and others physically. They ease the pain by supporting me as I limp along the dark road I suddenly find myself traversing.

During the Midnight Hours of silence and throughout the day while lost in my thoughts, I can't get the words *And yet* out of my mind. When Pastor Mike Campbell spoke at Michael's funeral service, he explained how two truths or realities that at face value appear to be in opposition to one another can actually exist at the same time within the same situation. This concept is often beyond our comprehension. He explained that, yes, we *will* miss Michael. Yes, there *will* be great pain. Yes, the pain *is* real *and* validated. *And yet*, God is still loving, merciful, and full of goodness, tender mercies, and abundant grace. *And yet* whispers to me.

I read in Psalm 6:6–9: "I am weary with my groaning; all night I make my bed swim; I drench my couch with tears. My eye wastes away because of grief; it grows old because of all my enemies. Depart from me, all you workers of iniquity." (Here comes another "and yet" or "but God.") "For the Lord" (and yet He) "has heard the voice of my weeping. The Lord has heard my supplication" (NKJV).

David says it again in Psalms 22:14–15 and 19: "I am poured out like water, and all My bones are out of joint; My heart is like wax; it has melted within Me. My strength is dried up like a potsherd, and My tongue clings to My jaws; You have brought Me to the dust of death... But You, O LORD, do not be far from Me; O My Strength, hasten to help Me!" (NKJV). David feels all of these emotions, but he knows he can look to God. I paraphrase this Scripture in my mind as my thoughts cry out to God, "Here I am, Lord—cried up, dried up, a wreck, lost, miserable, and feeling so heavy my bones can barely carry me. And yet I turn to You, because I know You are able, despite how I may be feeling. You are still there."

The first several weeks after Michael's death, I often thought about these words from Psalms. Up until Michael's death, the emotions David describes felt unrealistic to me, too dramatic, or even too passionate for any real human being to experience. But talking to Adrienne one day, I told her I was hurting in a place so deep down inside me that I had not even known it existed. My cries had turned into moans from somewhere deep in my belly, just as David describes. It turned my mind to him and these Scriptures that I had so often scanned over, thinking, *I can't relate. Move on.*

But now I get it.

My stomach muscles hurt from the deep cries and moaning. At times my muscles even convulse, as if I were sick to my stomach. These sudden moments of indescribable pain and tears continue to crush me as the wave train of grief relentlessly hits. Each blow makes me feel as if it's punching every bit of life out of me. For months I've hurt deep inside my soul, where no amount of crying, eating, drinking, or resting can ease the suffering.

Even once the wave train begins to weaken, my tears still overtake me like a sudden tidal wave. Every time I'm hit, it brings the recognition that Michael is no longer by my side. The valley is pitch black, and I don't know from one day to the next where my next step will take me.

And yet, the Lord is the lifter of my head and my rock.

CHAPTER 3

A Seascape of Grief

No one ever told me that grief felt so like fear. I am not
afraid, but the sensation is like being afraid. The same
fluttering in the stomach, the same restlessness, the
yawning. I keep on swallowing. At other times it feels like
being mildly drunk, or concussed. There is a sort of invisible
blanket between the world and me. I find it hard to take in
what anyone says. Or perhaps, hard to want to take it in. It is
so uninteresting. Yet I want the others to be about me.

—C. S. LEWIS, *A GRIEF OBSERVED*

T HE WEEK MICHAEL DIED A friend gave me a copy of *A Grief
Observed* by C. S. Lewis. I am stunned by how all of my physical
symptoms line up so completely with those he wrote about.
My body feels as if it has been stricken with fear, but without
an object to be fearful of. Lewis writes that he keeps yawning
and swallowing involuntarily. I feel exactly this way. Sometimes my tongue keeps swallowing and I can't make it stop,
and at other times I feel the need to swallow but my throat is
paralyzed and it's impossible. The stronger the wave of grief,
the more paralyzed my body feels. I have periods during the

day when I'm able to focus on the life that needs to continue moving forward, while at other moments the feelings completely wash over me. The restlessness and the fluttering in my stomach occur mostly at night, but also during business meetings about the accident or insurance, and sometimes in unexpected moments—like spotting a photograph of the two of us when I'm not looking for it.

Fear's symptoms began that awful night in February, in the blink of an eye.

My windows are open because the weather is so pleasant. Michael Anthony is sleeping in our king-size bed with me, as he occasionally does on the rare nights Michael is out of town. Michael is going to be gone only one night.

Michael Anthony and I awake to the dogs barking from the laundry room below my bedroom. I ignore it for a few minutes, but they keep barking. We then hear voices rise up through the open windows. I jump up and look out the second-story window overlooking the front patio. I see an unfamiliar car parked in front of my house. I grab the phone and dial 911 while checking my security pad to make sure the alarm is on. The pad has been malfunctioning, and I'm not able to get it to set or even to get the emergency alarm to go off. With 911 on the phone, I look out the window and notice two people standing at my front door. One of them is an officer. While talking to the operator, I loudly ask the figures through the window screen to identify themselves. The man tells me he's with the Hinds County sheriff's department. The woman identifies herself as someone representing Tunica County.

Immediately, I can't swallow.

Michael is spending the night in Tunica doing marketing calls in north Mississippi. He has more meetings planned for the morning before heading home for a dinner engagement. We've been foster parents to a little boy for the past ten months and planned a dinner with his biological parents. The custody hearing is in two days, and he will be going back to them.

I tell the operator, who is waiting on the phone, that I do not need her, tell Michael Anthony to stay in bed, grab my robe, and fly down to the front door.

As I open the front door, my ears begin burning. I hold the door only slightly ajar to see the faces of these two messengers staring blankly back at me. The male officer says, "Are you Mrs. Michael Barranco?" *Yes.* "Is this 425 Glenway Drive?" *Yes.* Their faces appear blank with fear of speaking.

Then the woman speaks: "We are here to report a fatality."

The rest is a blur, but I remember her saying he's been in a car accident and the police pronounced him dead upon arrival at the scene.

From this point on, I feel every bit of my blood drop down to my feet. My whole body feels paralyzed, just like it does under extreme fear. I cannot move a muscle on my face. I have to focus my whole body just to make my throat muscles do what they usually do instinctively. I have the need to swallow, but at the same time my mouth has gone suddenly and completely dry. I am suffocating.

I immediately think it's a mistake—someone has stolen his new car and possibly the body is unrecognizable, so they just assumed it's he who died in the crash. My heart is reaching for any lifeline.

"Are there any children in the house?"

The fear feeling intensifies as I realize all that is at stake. I reply while looking into their eyes with desperation for help, "Four...three of our own and a five-year-old foster child."

They ask if they can come inside while I make a phone call to the police commander in the Tunica office and also call a family member. I cannot think. I cannot speak. I cannot swallow. I don't even feel as if I'm breathing. When I am asked a question, my mouth and throat cannot form words. All I can seem to say is "Um," in a higher-than-normal, frightened pitch.

Those feelings continued for the rest of that day and have lingered on at different levels of intensity throughout all of my days since that early morning. I want to get beyond that memory. I want to *not* remember every detail. I want to forget the faces of the officials at my door. I want to forget the sound of the dogs barking in the early morning hours.

During these times of profound fear, I frequently quote 2 Timothy 1:7 to myself: "For God has not given us a spirit of fear, but of power and of love and of a sound mind" (NKJV). I taught these words to my children from the time they could talk. Every day I step back and recognize the fear I'm feeling— I face it, acknowledge it, and then discern what is reality and what truly is fear. I use the power of "a sound mind" God gave me. I wouldn't be able to walk this road of grief, in the valley of the shadow of death, without the understanding and relationship I have with Jesus Christ, my Comforter.

Yes, though I walk through the [deep, sunless] valley of the shadow of death, I will fear *or* dread no evil, for You are with me; Your rod [to protect] and Your staff [to guide], they comfort me. (Psalm 23:4 AMPC)

Over the days and months that follow, waves of grief continue to wash over me—crashing in, receding out, crashing in, and receding out. Each time they wash over me, part of my heart and strength are pulled out of me, sucked into the current to be swept away into the violent riptide. Unlike the sea, the waves are unpredictable and come at me from different directions. Striking in quick succession, they don't have to wait for the previous wave to recede before they crash forward again.

Facing each wave individually was the only way I could brace myself and endure the continual onslaught. During the short periods of recessions, I compartmentalized the waves by writing about the severity of each one, how it affected me, what I learned about life from the blow, and where I experienced the pain. I recorded the days in an effort to remember where I had been when the wave hit and how I got back on my feet after each one. No matter how hard they hit, slowly and deliberately I rose to my feet, reestablished my footing, and prepared for what might hit next. I even tried to anticipate the direction they might come from. Often, they returned only to hit me with the exact same force and wound me in the exact same place. At other times, they were less severe or wounded me in places I didn't know existed.

As I wrote my way through the grief, I numbered the days of the wave train, with day one being the day I was informed of Michael's death. Doing this enabled me to see the big picture and discover the patterns of strong waves and the smaller, less debilitating ones. Finally, I could see that the waves were hitting farther and farther apart until, one day, the water was calm. Waves were lapping in with the gentle pull of the tide, like a calm morning after a night storm at the beach. But the debris from the storm lay everywhere around us, limply floating in the sea or washed up on the shore like bodies on a battlefield.

As I cautiously walked through the debris, I began to pick up pieces of my heart as I recognized them. I picked up shards of my life. I picked up memories I wanted to keep. I even picked up my children, as they were washed up on the beach as well. We were alive, but barely. I tightly held on to all of these things, pulling them into my chest as I retreated into the only place I felt safe: my own private world of grief.

Grief is deep. It's shocking. It's complex. It's dark, lonely, and unpredictable.

DAY 22

Random Grief

I've had an arduous week filled with necessary business meetings with insurance companies, doctors, Boy Scout troop leaders, Social Security personnel, financial planners, and more. I have grieved for Michael through every bit of it. The heaviness of all of the meetings and discussing all of the issues is much harder than I'm sure it appears. Anytime I discuss business matters, the accident, insurance, or anything else related to this event, my insides begin to burn. It starts in the pit of my stomach, then the heat radiates up to my ears, and eventually my ears are ringing. It's as if I'm on fire. I cannot put into words the emotions I feel during these times. Words that come to mind are lonely, exposed, fearful, petrified, vulnerable, scared, consumed—like a child who is lost at an amusement park might feel.

Many friends prayed for me this week, and God answered the prayers by helping me take one thing at a time so that each meeting wasn't as bad as I had anticipated it might be. Oh, I still cried plenty of tears and felt the weight, but it was slightly bearable. I feel like my grieving was random this week. I couldn't put my finger on any one thing, but I felt the grief everywhere. Everywhere I turned, there it was—even in the pharmacy.

I was inside Walgreens picking up some medicine for Julia when the pharmacist asked if I had a new insurance card, because the one they had on file didn't work. I told her yes and pulled out my new one. She asked if there were others insured that she could go ahead and add to make the changes on the computer. I told her yes, my three children. She wrote down their names with the last one being Michael Anthony, Jr. Noticing the Jr., she asked if their father was insured on this card as well. I answered, "No. He recently died. It was in his name but was changed over to mine." I had to answer her quickly, but as soon as I said it, I felt as if I had just been blindsided. With heat quickly rising from my stomach and my heart pounding in my chest, I was suddenly searching for my pack of tissues in my purse to catch the tears streaming down my cheeks.

Each morning this week as I dressed and anticipated the meetings of the day, I missed Michael's strength. We anchored one another. I felt the weight of carrying out these responsibilities without him. I cried while I got ready. When I can't pinpoint the feelings I am having, I cry more. This week, I simply missed Michael and needed him all across the board. Random grief.

The book I am occasionally reading now is Wendell Berry's Hannah Coulter. I picked it up recently, and the page that I "happened" to have marked held this profound thought, which is timely for me this week: Hannah tells the story of losing her husband in the war while living with her in-laws. She writes, "I began to know my story then. Like everybody's, it was going to be the story of living in the absence of the dead. What is the thread that holds it all together? Grief, I thought for a while... But grief is not a force and has no power to hold. You only bear it. Love is what carries you."

Love is carrying me—Michael's love, God's love, and the love of those who remain. This thought helps me turn my random grief to a focused love of a lifetime.

DAY 24

Oceans, Rivers, and Lakes

I rarely know when a wave is coming, why it hit me so hard, or how long I'm going to stumble on my knees, gasping for air. I keep thinking how all of this is like natural water sources. Water sustains me, refreshes me, and cleans me, but at the same time it can sweep me off my feet, causing me to stumble or choke, and it also has the power to suffocate me or even steal my life.

Sometimes I feel as if I'm in the ocean and a big wave has crashed over me, catching me off guard and knocking me off my feet. It takes my breath away for a moment. I struggle to stand as the undertow reaches at my legs to pull me back down, but I recover to my feet again. At other times I feel as if I am standing in a river with a strong, rushing current. Every step is heavy and labored as I feel the weight of the water pushing against me. I'm not able to withstand the force for very long; I'm easily swept off my feet and carried away in the current for a while before I find something to grab on to and then pull myself back out of the water.

Even lake water has its own challenges. The water is heavier, swimming is harder, and I can't always see what is lurking around me. Most days I feel as if I am struggling to tread water in a lake. I typically feel the weight and pressure on all sides, and then, like a dam, the pressure is too much. I begin to go under, but then the floodgate lifts to release some of the force that has been building on the inside. Once the tears release, I feel better, but exhausted from the struggle.

Drinking my green tea in bed this morning, I pick up a stack of note cards sitting on my nightstand that my close friend Beth gave me one at a time over the first several weeks after Michael's death. Each card has a Scripture written on it. I come across this verse that gives me hope:

When you pass through the waters,
I will be with you;
and when you pass through the rivers,
they will not sweep over you. (Isaiah 43:2 NIV)

God's timing to remind me of this promise is perfect.
What a poignant truth of the love my Heavenly Father has for me.

It doesn't matter where I turn, where I go, or how hard I'm sucked into the current. He will be with me, after me, and for me—lifting me out of the waters and allowing me to catch my breath.

DAY 26

Dirty Laundry

I fell behind on washing clothes the first few weeks after Michael's death. When I finally washed a load of darks, I found Michael's Boy Scout pants at the bottom of our laundry bag. The weekend before the accident, he had gone on a Boy Scout campout with Michael Anthony. He typically did not unpack his bag immediately upon returning from camping. Somehow, those pants did not make it into the wash that Monday morning and had been hidden under a pair of my jeans in the laundry bag. When I spotted them, I slowly lifted them out of the bag, looked them over, and dug my hands into every pocket, hoping to find any little trace of what he had done while he was camping. I was disappointed to find them all empty.

Throughout our marriage, I did laundry on Mondays. I never wanted to do laundry throughout the week. The kids knew when they woke up on Monday mornings to bring their sorted laundry down to the laundry room. The girls run their own clothes through the cycles, Michael Anthony does his own sorting and folding, and I have always washed the boys' and mine.

I was notified about Michael's accident in the early hours of a Wednesday morning. His accident had taken place about ten thirty the night before, within minutes of our "good night, I love you" phone conversation.

Later in the day, on that tragic Wednesday, I found myself trying to find a crumpled, used T-shirt so I could smell him. But all of his laundry was clean. I was mad that I couldn't find anything showing a sign of his recent life. I grabbed two of his long-sleeved T-shirts, which he loved wearing at night, and sat on our bed. I wrapped them around my neck, put the arms in front of my nose, and cried like I had never cried before in my life. I was drowning.

The softness of the shirts satisfied the need for his recent life because that softness was why he loved to sleep in them. The children and I have slept in them many times, looking for even a trace of his scent. I scanned through his dress clothes, looking for any worn dress shirts. Touching them somehow made me feel like I was hugging him for the last time.

I miss his dirty clothes. I washed his last piece of dirty laundry, folded the pants with tenderness, and hung them with his uniform shirt. He was a Scout to the end.

DAY 38

Heart Broken

The LORD is close to the brokenhearted
and saves those who are crushed in spirit. (Psalm 34:18 NIV)

For the first time in my life, my heart is broken. I believe I must have lived a charmed life by not having my heart broken before now. My heart was preserved and whole when I gave it to Michael on our wedding day in 1987. I gladly gave it to him, knowing he would protect it—and he did. We carried part of each other's hearts. When he died, part of my heart seemed to die with him. My heart is breaking by not having that part of my heart near me.

While out shopping recently, I came across a print that read TO MY HEART, YOU HOLD THE KEY. *I took a deep breath as tears filled my eyes. Standing motionless, I soaked in that thought for a moment. Not everyone allows his or her heart to be unlocked, or ever finds the person with the right key. I held Michael's key and he held mine. We were the gatekeepers of one another's hearts and made sure nothing got in that did not go through us first.*

Losing Michael is also heartbreaking because I shared countless memories with him that only he knew. Several weeks ago, I was talking to someone and sharing a memory about one of the kids when they were little. I was overcome with the thought that I'm the only one who has that memory now. Just to be able to sit with the family, look at Michael, and say, "Remember when Mia would run, not walk, every time she went to her bedroom? You could hear her feet speed up on the hardwood floors as she turned the corner." "Remember when Julia loved to lie in her baby bed and look at magazines, a whole stack at a time?" "Remember when Michael Anthony climbed out of his crib every night before the door was even closed behind you?" There is no one to say "remember when" with anymore. I am the keeper of the memories now.

Sometimes I feel as if the words broken heart *or* widow *are hanging in front of me like the scarlet letter. Even though no one sees it, I feel as if they do. Several times over the past month I thought I was getting a sore throat. I realized one day that I was experiencing something new. There is an ever-present lump in my throat; I am ready to cry at any second. It's large and sometimes feels stuck down in the bottom of my throat, as if I've just swallowed a big, hard air bubble. Where does that lump come from, anyway? I've had a lump in my throat for a little over five weeks now. I keep swallowing and* crying, but it doesn't seem to go anywhere. It's a broken heart. It swells before it can heal.

The part of my heart I gave to Michael will never return, but I know my God can heal my wound. He has provided a promise in the Scriptures to fit my exact need. I have everything surrounding this Scripture underlined, but this particular verse is not, because I have never needed to remember it before now:

He heals the brokenhearted
and binds up their wounds. (Psalm 147:3 NIV)

DAY 42

Blindsided

I was almost enjoying myself a few days ago in my favorite beachside gift shop. Earlier that day I'd spent several hours with the children on the beach doing absolutely nothing. But while in the gift shop, I looked up and saw this beautifully framed poster hanging on the wall with a quote from Winnie-the-Pooh. "If you live to be a hundred, I want to live to be a hundred minus one day, so I never have to live without you." Suddenly I couldn't breathe. The wave crashed over me with unexpected force—blindsided me. I had assumed Michael and I would grow that old together, never having to live one without the other. Frozen for a few minutes, I stood there regaining my composure before I could turn around to face anyone in the store.

It happened again last night while I was watching a Christian comedy video with some friends and my children. This time I saw it coming in the near distance. I had seen most of this video before, but we watched one of the acts I'd never seen. It was clean and fun, but the flippant attitude toward life, love, and relationships began to feel so ungrateful and careless. The comedian was making jokes about the marriage relationship, mostly laughing at himself but also making references to "this is what wives do and this is what men think." It hurt me. He does not know what it can really be like. He doesn't know how much love and respect is possible. He doesn't know what he is missing. He doesn't know what he has. How dare he make jokes about something so treasured as a relationship between a husband and wife? What a missed opportunity.

I had to excuse myself and go to another room to "get a drink of water" in order to shift my thoughts. My marriage with Michael was too special to listen to someone degrade marriage in any way, shape, or form.

I now choose movies, music, and topics of conversation with much trepidation. I'm not typically one to get caught off guard about many things, but it happens frequently now. I could prepare myself, but it won't stop the surge of emotions. I wouldn't even say that everything is sitting right below the surface, ready to rise at any given moment. The emotions, the hurts, are all still on the surface. Seeing the blow coming doesn't make it hurt any less. It simply gives me a second to catch my breath or tighten up before the wave smacks up against me. After a blindsided hit, I literally lose my breath for a few moments. I feel the pain and shock, and finally, breathe deeply before struggling to get back on my feet.

DAY 54

Adrenaline Crash

I've been operating on adrenaline simply to survive—meeting with people I need to see, taking care of financial business, wrapping up things with Michael's business, continuing to take care of issues concerning the visitation and the funeral service (reading letters and cards, writing thank-you notes, which are nearing a thousand, getting copies of audio and video recordings of the service to those who want it, etc.), running my household to the best of my abilities (which are not up to par yet), keeping up with my kids' schedules, planning for the future, making necessary decisions, being available to help with our foster child (who is now home with his family)—and grieving through all of it.

I've been experiencing physical anxiety—my heart pounds in my chest to the point that I think it will leap out of my body. This is what keeps me awake at night. While I am in bed, it's easy for my mind to drift back to the moment when I heard someone knocking at our door at three thirty in the morning. I keep hearing the words "We are here to report a fatality." My heart goes from normal to pounding in a split second. I force my thoughts in other directions and take deep breaths. My doctor told me this is my body in its "fight or flight" mode. Because I am not literally fighting or fleeing, the anxiety builds in me. He told me that allowing myself to cry hard and talk to people through my tears is crucial to helping my body deal with this response. My daytime energy comes from sheer adrenaline, but it doesn't know how to turn off at night. I've had to take a very light sleep aid to allow my body and mind time without the adrenaline rush working full throttle.

Last week, after returning from a beach trip, I decided to stop taking the sleep aid because I didn't like the way it made me feel during the day. I slept all right that night. Then, over the next two days, both Michael Anthony and I began to experience our adrenaline crashing.

We are tired all of the time. He allows himself simply to lie on the couch and do nothing, which is not his nature at all. One day he took his time looking through a scrapbook my aunt put together with news articles about Michael that I had saved over the years. After looking at it, he went to lie down on the couch and slept over two hours. He even turned down an invitation to spend the night out and go turkey hunting so he could rest and spend time with family. This was when I realized he was seriously tired and his adrenaline rush was crashing.

I walk around feeling foggy, as if I've just woken up from a long, deep nap even though I rarely sleep. My eyes feel tired and burn. Phone conversations and e-mails take too much energy. And then finally, last night, I slept deeply and naturally, without medication. My body is beginning to relent. Am I finally getting some relief from the adrenaline crash? Is the fight almost over?

I could have written this verse in Psalm 3:5, where King David is crying out to God for help with his troubles while affirming what God does for him: "I lay down and slept; I wakened again, for the Lord sustains me" (AMPC).

I feel that we are just slightly, ever so slightly, beginning to stand on our feet again. I hope the fact that we are actually tired is a good sign. Our bodies are resting. It will be a while, a long while, before we are all fully rested, but experiencing our bodies beginning to let down has been like being able to breathe without reminding ourselves to do so.

DAY 62

It's a Long Road

Have I mentioned how hard this is? I mean really hard. Every minute of every day is hard. Every breath I take is hard. My breathing patterns have not been the same since Michael died. My breath is always shallow, and at the same time I feel like there is something heavy weighing on my chest. All day long I tell myself, "Take a deep breath." Throughout the day another reminder: "Just breathe. Inhale deeply. Now exhale."

Until now, I had no idea how it feels to lose someone you love with all of your heart. Lord, forgive me if I was ever not compassionate enough, or didn't show mercy long enough, to someone in my walk of life who was grieving as I am now.

I cry daily. Sometimes a little here and a little there, and sometimes I still cry hard. Last week was a tough week, but Friday was the hardest of all. I'm not sure why. Maybe it was because the whole week had been tough and I was exhausted, or maybe it was because I had a close friend sit down with me to ask questions, listen, and allow me to cry. Maybe it was because it was the beginning of Easter weekend, and Michael always took off from work on Good Friday. It was an important day for us as we began a whole weekend of celebrating Jesus Christ and all that He accomplished through His life, death, and resurrection. But then again, maybe it was simply because grieving is a very long, painful road.

There are no shortcuts on this journey. It is a journey that must be taken slowly. I must experience the pain, meditate on the loss, sit down occasionally when I am weak, and then slowly stand and move when I am able. I am trying to see and feel everything along the way.

I seem to fall apart when life gets too busy and I feel rushed or pushed along the road. I still need time to sit still and be quiet every day. I feel robbed at the end of the day if I don't set apart a time to be still. Sometimes my quiet moments come at unexpected times and in unexpected places.

Like today, in the closet.

I pick out a tie for Michael Anthony to wear to church. It's the Easter morning rush. Since Michael's clothes are still in the closet, I decide to pull out one of his ties because he had a beautiful collection. To him, the right tie made an outfit, like the perfect pair of shoes does for a woman. I enter the closet with my mind focused on the task at hand and look through all the choices. I feel my movements slow down. I take my time looking at the ties, touching them. I remember what he wore with each one, how handsome he looked in suits, how he beamed when I told him so, and how important the right tie was to him—how strong he looked when he wore one.

It's perfectly quiet in the closet. All I hear is the lightbulb faintly ringing above me. I linger in the moment. I long to see him dressing for church and tying the knot in his tie.

I emerge with two fabulous ties and feel as if I've just experienced a little rest stop on the road of grief. I let Michael Anthony pick the one he likes best. Thankfully, I know how to tie a tie from when it was fashionable for girls to wear skinny ties in the eighties. I don't tie it as well as his father would have, but it does the job.

It is a long road. I hope my friends and family can hang in there with me for the long haul. I need them to allow me to take my time. I need them to handle me with care, listen to me (but not give too much advice), love me, pray often for me, join me when I stop to rest, and remember Michael with me. Some say his death is heaven's gain (and that is not what I want to hear), but we are still on this earthly journey, and it hurts.

DAY 78

Mother's Day

I woke up feeling like it was any other Sunday. We were ten minutes late for the eight o'clock service, like any other Sunday, and we all sat together in church, like any other Sunday. We got ready and left without any fanfare. It wasn't until we arrived at the country club for lunch that the grief came tumbling down.

I walk into the lobby, and several young women greet me. Years ago I coached them in cheerleading. I was their mentor, and they were my unofficial adopted teenage daughters. But now they stand before me as young women, grieving and looking for the right words to say. After some hugs and condolences, I walk into the main dining room. I go straight to the buffet to get my food. I don't know why I didn't plan ahead for this wave. I've been here countless times over the last twenty-four years, but everything is different now. I didn't see it coming.

Here I am, standing in the very room where Michael and I celebrated our marriage. At this very moment, I'm standing where Michael and I had our first dance. Right behind me, the Andy Hardwick Trio played while Michael held my hand and sang Sam & Dave's "When Something Is Wrong with My Baby." The same place where he sang James Brown's "I Feel Good" and every person on the waitstaff came out and lined the walls to hear "this white man sing like nobody's business." Everyone flooded the dance floor. Did this waiter helping me right now witness us celebrating that day? Suddenly, the food is no longer appealing to me. A familiar lead weight appears in the pit of my stomach. In my heart I cry to God, "Father, why do I have to experience this? Why me—out of all these people? Rescue me! Bring me some relief!"

Numb and unaware of my footsteps, I make my way to our table. It's as though a heavy blanket has been thrown over me, just as C. S. Lewis describes in A Grief Observed. I sit down and want to crawl into a hole and cry my eyes out, but at the same time I don't want to cry in this crowd. There are hundreds of people here, and at least half of them know Michael or me. The big lump in the deep part of my throat reappears. Everyone is talking but I'm an outsider, lost in another world. The tears tip at the edge of my lower lids, ready to spill over at any second.

I try thinking about something else, but I can't push the memories away. Right behind me was where we served the virgin strawberry daiquiris and champagne. Over there was the table with the miniature muffulettas from New Orleans. Two tables over, we cut the wedding cake, and next to that was the groom's cake—Italian cream cake with little Italian flags stuck all over it. I struggle to talk to my family sitting at the table with me. I decide it's best not to make eye contact with anyone. Looking into people's eyes always brings the tears. As people walk by our table, I act as if I don't see them. Sometimes it works and sometimes it doesn't. I barely eat any of my salad. I move it around the plate a little bit, but hardly touch my lunch.

I desperately miss Michael. I want to hold his hand and hear him sing to me again. I want to dance with him again. I want him to hold me and tell me everything is going to be okay. I want to see him gaze into my eyes with that loving look he always gave me.

I'm relieved it's finally time to leave. As we walk out, I focus my eyes on the floor in front of me so I don't have to greet anyone. Once outside, my brother Kyle, who lives in South Africa, calls on my sister Jerri's cell phone. He wants to wish us a happy Mother's Day. We try some small talk and then he says he just wants to tell me happy Mother's Day. I hear the concern and love in his voice, which makes me want to cry even more—I choose to get off the phone as quickly as possible.

I spent the rest of the afternoon lost in my memories of all of the poems and songs Michael wrote for me on Mother's Day. I remember how he would bring me a special hot drink as I got ready for church and then say, "So, how is my amazing little mama?" or put his arm around me at church and look at me with a smile and pride in his eyes. He made me feel special every day of the year. He knew how to celebrate me and celebrate life. I'm thankful for these memories in the midst of this numbing grief.

DAY 104

Discombobulated

I was rather melancholy most of today. I felt out of sorts in all different areas. Michael and I used to enjoy using the word discombobulated. *Not only is it fun to say, but it also conveys its particular meaning simply by the way it rolls off your tongue. It can mean confused and disconcerted, or unsettled, thrown off balance. I felt discombobulated today.*

Michael's absence is obvious in so many places that it sometimes causes me to feel awkward, unsettled, and confused—discombobulated.

How do I respond in this moment without him in it? Where is this person who understood my every thought? Countless times today, my mind was far away as I thought about Michael and how different my life is now without him in it. There is a word in the book of Psalms that my sister Julie uses often—it describes what I did repeatedly today: selah, *which means "pause and think about it." It seemed as if the whole day was filled with* selah *moments. I'm getting fairly good at crying on the inside or hiding my tears that well up in my eyes. Today I was a master at it. No one had any idea how distant I was from the present.*

Michael Anthony played in his first tennis tournament today. All of the boys playing had a dad with them, watching with a coach's intensity. Michael Anthony, on the other hand, had me, Julia, a friend of his from out of town, a friend of mine who plays tennis and warmed him up before his match, two uncles, the church administrator, and a man from our church. I wanted to make sure he felt supported, so I made sure he had a larger cheering section than the other boys playing. Despite his number of fans, the weight of his father's absence was obvious not only in his face, but also in the way he carried his body on the court. He held his head low most of the time, his shoulders slumped, and his feet nearly dragged as he walked. He didn't win but played some great points. With every ball he missed or double fault he made, he gave up more and more. If the ball was out of reach, he didn't even attempt to get his racquet on it. It was as if he was thinking, What's the point? *He's lost most of his will to fight.*

I wanted to go up to the referee or the dad of the young boy he was playing and say, "Have mercy—he has had a rough three months. Not only is this his first tournament, but he just lost his dad, his best friend, his 'Bud.' Can't he earn some points just for the fight of being here?" I felt discombobulated watching him work this out alone.

When we got home, he wanted his favorite salad. I was happy to make it for him. But as I pulled out the salad spinner, my actions began to move in slow motion, involuntarily; my heart saddened as my mind went to all of the times I'd used the salad spinner for family dinners when Michael was still with us. I haven't cooked in three months. People have generously brought us meals. I haven't wanted to cook. I used to make salads every day. The last time I used the salad spinner was Michael's last meal with us on Monday night, February 21. I made manicotti and a salad. Our family dinners almost always included a fresh salad. The salad spinner reminded me of life in the kitchen with Michael in the house. I took my time. Selah. I paused and thought about it.

After serving Michael Anthony the salad, I realized I needed to buy some perennials to plant next week in the garden. (Actually, I won't do the planting. I still cannot do it without Michael.) This made me think of how different my Saturdays are now. It's strange not working my weekend plans around his plans. Michael always had high expectations of Saturdays. He was constantly motivated and brought me along for the ride. We each had things we wanted to accomplish, but we stepped into each other's tasks to help whenever it was necessary. Today, I was able simply to leave and go get plants. Most people would see this as a positive, but it made me feel discombobulated. He would have been working in the garden and then later would have called me at the gardening store to add some things to my list or to ask my opinion on what he was doing. I'm now the only one working on Saturdays—it accentuates my loneliness. I paused and thought about how different, awkward, and quiet it felt for a Saturday.

The afternoon brought the girls' dance recital. They both take hip-hop. I was overwhelmed at the beginning of their dance number and fought the tears from breaking through the dam. I had to blink them away to keep my vision from blurring. I could not believe the years that had passed and how hip-hop had come back around in our lives. I taught hip-hop dance and choreographed for groups for almost twenty years. I stopped teaching before Julia was old enough to take one of my classes. Mia started taking hip-hop classes from me when she was nine. Now, after I've retired from teaching dance, my girls are carrying on my love for the dance. Michael would have been proud watching them dance like their mama onstage. I was proud. They were enjoying themselves, and I understood the joy of dancing they were experiencing. Selah. I paused and thought about the passing of years.

After the recital, I took them out to eat at a neighborhood restaurant, along with Jennings, my twenty-six-year-old niece. We sat at a table on the outdoor patio of the restaurant, which is located in an old brick building that was once a school. It was recently restored as a multi-use building. I looked up at its exterior brick walls. My thoughts immediately went to Michael. I noticed the way the edges of the building met, and I knew what Michael would have said about the building: it was done right. He always pointed out architectural details and explained to me what was right about them and what was wrong. He wanted me to know and appreciate the difference. I remember when we took all of the kids to Italy, along with his parents, and he taught us about architecture all of the time. Classical architecture was his favorite. I think he felt this way because it's balanced, orderly, brilliant, strong, and timeless. The sight of a brick wall brought all of these thoughts. Selah.

There were many times today when my thoughts drifted back to my life with Michael. Tonight I'm extremely tired and want to go to *bed quickly to end this day of melancholy reminiscing, a whole day of feeling discombobulated, out of balance, unsettled. My Saturdays may feel like this for a while.*

A grief observed. I observed my grief with a fierce intensity. I tried to write down every detail as accurately as I could. I saw my grief as something significant, and I wanted to learn all that it had for me. I took in all of its moving parts and tried to create some sense of order by facing the parts one at a time. I absorbed every wave of grief that hit my heart. Soaked, drenched by grief, I kept moving forward with labored, deliberate steps. I knew that one day, even though it felt as if this journey through the raging waters would never end, eventually the waves would subside to the point where I could turn around and gaze back to see a seascape of grief and know that I had made it through the storm.

CHAPTER 4

The Midnight Hour

We must look beyond the shadows; night is not the
time for action but for repose. The light of reason only
intensifies the darkness of faith; and the rays that can
pierce it must come from on high.

—Jean-Pierre de Caussade,
The Sacrament of the Present Moment

THE DOOR STOOD OPEN, PURPOSEFULLY left ajar for twenty-five years. Our lives converged with an accumulated force ready to release in that first moment the door flung open to our lives together. Movements of life breezed through its framework, sounds of joy echoed from both directions, freedom floated easily back and forth. The open door led me to places I had never been before. Once the door opened, it was like watching the sunrise again and again, continually being surprised by its creativity, its miraculous renewal powers. Because of the open door, a fresh beginning was always available. An endless future. Inexhaustible dreams. Immeasurable desires. Michael and I held hands through the door. We traversed back and

53

forth, reaching forward and back to glean and savor the moments.

As with all tsunamis, no signs of an impending storm were seen that day. No warning signals. No change in the temperature. No time to take shelter. The only change was from day to night. The sun disappeared. It was the Midnight Hour.

Doors are typically shut during the Midnight Hour, but ours was kept ajar. Freedom and security (ironically) prevailed with our open-door policy—but on February 22, the door slammed shut with power and a vengeance, as with the end of a relationship. Michael on one side of the door. I on the other. He in the light. I in the dark.

And so began my walk alone through the Midnight Hour.

The Midnight Hour—the darkest hour—is silent and cold, the turning point when one day ends and another begins. The Midnight Hour is lonely—frightening at times. One can hear the silence more clearly. Feel the darkness more profoundly.

The Midnight Hour—my long period of repose following Michael's death. It was a cold, silent journey. It seemed as if I would never come through it. I craved the moment when I would feel the sun on my face again, the dawning of a new day. Another open door. But it was endless days—weeks, months, years—of the Midnight Hour. As Jean-Pierre de Caussade writes, "The light of reason only intensifies the darkness of faith; and the rays that can pierce it must come from on high." And so I waited for the rays to pierce through the darkness.

In the Midnight Hour, God was silent most of the time—present, but silent.

When Michael died, I felt forsaken. I thought of it as "extreme separation," not solely physical because we were now on different sides of the door, but also spiritual separation from Michael, similar to what Jesus felt on the cross when God separated Himself from him. I felt this extreme separation not only from my husband, but also from God at the same time. They had both been my lifelines, and it felt as if I had been cut away from them simultaneously. Michael was physically gone. There could be no more communication. With God, He was present, but surprisingly quiet, not saying a word.

My friend Frank, who is also well acquainted with grief, wrote me during those early months about the separation even Jesus experienced while he hung dying on the cross. A feeling of being forsaken, a period of no communication with God, when he physically felt like he needed Him the most.

Frank wrote, "He felt it acutely when he was pouring out his life and his blood on the cross for our sins. At that point and time, the Father had to leave him, separated from everyone and everything, on the cross so the sacrifice would be complete. He cried out, 'My God, My God, why have you forsaken me?' There was no reply from heaven."

After losing Michael, there have been many months of feeling completely numb. I have absolutely nothing to say to God—and He has nothing to say to me. Alone in my bedroom, where I continue to escape from life and face my grief, the painful silence continues. It's as if a vacuum has sucked every last bit of sound out of my room. Only God and I, simply sitting here—in utter silence. I know God is still the same, but my circumstances have changed, and the way we communicate has changed. I don't feel like He's gone or has left me behind, but I feel as if I'm in the "there was no reply from heaven" stage. And the silence is deafening.

Just as best friends or spouses often sit together in silence with one another because of the depth of the love and understanding between them, God and I sit in silence. Sometimes there are no words needed or no words that can be said. Some of the best comfort I receive from friends is a loving embrace and a knowing look into my eyes that says, "I love you; I am hurting, too. I am here for you." But it's all unspoken.

I've always enjoyed a two-way conversation with God. I talked to Him, and if I took time to listen, He talked to me. But now, in the Midnight Hour, we only sit quietly next to one another. What comfort can words bring, anyway? The loss is still here. I feel Him with me in spite of the silence. I feel the silent understanding. I don't hear answers or advice. Sometimes I feel comforted by the silence, and at other times I want to scream. I know He loves me and He hurts for me, but there is no reply from heaven, and quite frankly, I don't want to talk.

As I sit in silence in my bedroom, I wonder, *Should I say something to Him?* But there is nothing, so we continue sitting in silence. I listen every waking hour. The silence doesn't mean we are absent from one another. We're hurting, and have nothing to say. Even though God is silent, I hungrily depend on His presence. I have zero understanding or knowledge of what is happening in my life. I recognize that asking God to help me understand why this happened will not bring Michael back. Instead, I search for what I can learn about my life from the tragedy and what the new direction for my life is now.

Nanette and I attend a retreat in Colorado led by Ransomed

Heart Ministries and best-selling authors John and Stasi Eldredge. John says one simple statement that sticks with me. Regarding trying to understand something that we are going through or something God has asked us to do, he says, "Understanding is overrated!" We want to understand what God is doing so badly, but understanding doesn't usually change our circumstances or make the task any easier. In most instances, what do we ultimately gain by understanding? Nothing, really—so why not simply trust? "If God *is* for us who *can be* against us?" (Rom. 8:31 NKJV).

My situation forces me to trust God because He is bigger than what I can conceive. He knows the big picture—the picture I can't possibly grasp while walking through a dark storm. Even though I cannot always see the purpose God intends for me, I fight for it with determination and strive to discover it. I trust that my purpose for living will slowly become apparent to me, even in the silence.

<hr />

I focus on God's presence despite the silence. My life depends on it. I finally acknowledge His presence with a simple "Thank you." I tell Him the only thing I feel. No quoting Scriptures. No pleas for anything. Not even praise. I don't even have a beginning or an official "Amen" to the barely audible words that come out of my mouth. The silence finally breaks. I whisper, "Thank you."

I whisper these words in the true Midnight Hour. The irrepressible words hover in the darkness. The tears silently roll onto my pillow. On other evenings, following this first audible two-word prayer, I occasionally pray silently. My mouth remains mute, but, even still, only thankfulness rises out from my heart as it reaches for Him. "For the mouth speaks what the heart is full of" (Luke 6:45 NIV).

It's difficult for others to understand why "Thank you" is all I can say. Given my circumstances, even I don't understand it. My mouth, my heart, can't produce any other words. I silently thank Him for carrying me through each day, and then again for carrying me through each night. I thank Him for the life He's given me up to this point. I do have much for which I'm thankful, but beyond that, I simply don't know what to say to Him.

Aside from these "Thank you" silent prayers, the silence between God and me continues on.

Rick Warren, author of *The Purpose Driven Life,* states, "The most common mistake Christians make in worship today is seeking an *experience* rather than seeking God...God often removes our feelings so we won't depend on them." He goes on to say, "It is painful and disconcerting, but it is absolutely vital for the development of your faith." All of my feelings have been completely removed. There is no "experiencing God." I learn that He's present even if it doesn't feel like it. Even in complete silence.

My faith and the Scriptures are my bedrock and sole source of what little strength I scavenge. This morning, the wave train strikes me powerfully. I feel lonely and completely abandoned—I'm drowning in thoughts of missing Michael. Confusion and overpowering sadness settle on me.

Blurred and drenched, my eyes scan the room, taking in all

of the remnants of Michael. They land on a small picture on my nightstand, but then I spot the collection of Beth's note cards sitting atop my towering stack of to-be-read books. I reach for an index card. I read 1 Thessalonians 5:16–18: "Rejoice always, pray without ceasing, give thanks in all circumstances; for this is the will of God in Christ Jesus for you" (ESV)—I abruptly stop—"give thanks in all circumstances." I sob even more as an unexpected and overwhelming feeling of thankfulness washes over me. And in this agonizing moment, the thankfulness can only come from heaven.

Again—only thankfulness arises.

Thank you, God, for bringing Michael to me. Out of all the women in the world, You chose me. Thank you for giving me that privilege. Thank you for choosing me to be his wife here on this earth. Thank you for the life we had together. Thank you for the way he provided for our family. Thank you for the hard worker that he was. Thank you for his discipline. Thank you for his steadfast love. Thank you for his faithfulness. Thank you for his sweet spirit. Thank you for the children you gave me. Thank you for the father he was to our children. Thank you for his wisdom. Thank you for his guidance for our family. Thank you for his influence. Thank you for his integrity. Thank you for his voice.

I feel lifted, and yet exhausted after pouring out this spirit of thankfulness from my crushing heart. I feel connected to God and Michael's spirit at the same time. I temporarily breathe again. Sometimes a rush of tears and a wave of thankfulness overcome me while I'm in the shower. Maybe the water drenching my body gives me the feeling that my heart needs cleansing of its pain as well. I'm not in control of the thankfulness that springs forth in these moments. I can't explain it. In the flesh, who would be thankful right now? But God knows what I need. Each time I'm thankful, I gain a little more strength to carry on.

I desperately crave the solitude of my room. I feel cocooned here. I hide from the busy world here. I crave it because I sort my feelings here. I need the silence I find here. Most of all, I need to write here. My health depends on it.

The more I write, the more my blood pressure normalizes. The more I write, the less my heart pounds in my chest. The more I write, the more I breathe. The more I write, the more I sleep. The more I write, the more the weight of grief lifts from my chest. But getting the solitude I need isn't as easy as a trip up the stairs. I make my personal healing a priority and create the time.

As I look at my sister Julie one day while our eyes brim with tears, she tells me I've placed myself and my needs too low on the priority list. Since I'm a mother, it's natural to put the needs of my children first. But in a case such as death, it's imperative that I present a rested, healing self to my children, that I take care of me so I can take care of them. I plan ahead for my larger blocks of solitude. Slipping away here and there to my bedroom is not always enough. I proactively create a place for me in my life. Julie helps me plan periodic short getaways, no more than one to two hours away—like the one-day retreat in the guest bedroom of my friend Catherine.

It's a quiet and tranquil place—a room of beauty with rich brown heart-of-pine wood flooring, warm blue walls, and cascading blue silk curtains hanging just below the eleven-foot ceilings. It's a space where I sit with God, without any distractions. It's a space that nurtures me. Absorbing the ambience, I decide to write about something that recently caused an even deeper struggle in my heart, to the point where I actually stopped writing. I chose not to write about it at first because the place felt too deep and dark to share with anyone.

Oh, the loneliness of the Midnight Hour.

The intensified darkness became even more profoundly cold and silent.

This moment in my friend's nurturing guest bedroom is a sign that I'm slowly coming back up from the depths where I recently found myself. I crashed to an all-time low. It crept up on me for several days, but then suddenly I was drowning. The darkness was burying me alive. My body felt as if it had no weight or, conversely, that the weight of the world pressed all around me. I either floated through the motions of my household life without a single feeling, like an emotionless robot, or I laboriously moved through the tiniest task. My face, continually expressionless, felt incapable of making any change from the flat, empty glaze it wore. I could not smile. I did not want to talk. Life felt blank, bland, and completely, utterly, absent of joy.

The depth of this absence of joy is a first for me. I remind myself again, as before, "Breathe. Deeply." Am I even alive? I don't remember how it happened, but somehow I ended up on the phone with Julie. I broke down as I told her how empty I felt; any thread or remnant of joy was now gone—completely. She immediately took the kids out of the house and gave me the next three hours alone to work through this extreme low.

I was in a mental search for joy. I needed a grip on biblical joy. What does *joy* mean, anyway? What should it look like? Is it wrong for me not to feel or walk in joy at this time? I searched this great void. I went up to my bedroom while the house was empty and decided to write something—anything at all. I wasn't sure I could even write in my usual form, so I chose a poem:

Mysterious Joy

Empty   void   monotonous   blank
Duty   bland   continual   drudgery
Robotic expressionless motionless numbing
Invisible, concealed, hidden, covert

Stir it up, seek for it
Dig for it, fight for it
Uncover it, desire it . . . mysterious joy

Keep moving, lean forward, believe, trust
Presence, feeling
Absence, searching
Discovering, understanding . . . mysterious joy

Now, as I sit in the warm blue guest bedroom in Catherine's home, I comb through countless Scriptures and studies on joy. I write down all my thoughts. My conclusion is simple: I'm not in a place yet to feel, show, or walk out any *form* of joy—as we know joy. Then a verse finds me: "Be joyful in hope, patient in affliction, faithful in prayer" (Rom. 12:12 NIV). I think to myself, *I can be joyful in hope.* This does not require a physical joy; this is something I *can* do. I can be joyful in my certainty (my hope) of God's sovereignty. I can be joyful in my anticipation (my hope) of God's perfect plan for my life.

J. Hampton Keathley III said in a study on hope, "The Christian life, if it is grasped according to God's truth, is a magnificent obsession with an eternal hope, a hope that does not lead to an escapist attitude, but to the pursuit of life on a whole new dimension. It makes you bullish on the potentials of life as stewards of God. It gives us power to live courageously to be all God has called us to be in Christ."

I *do* have an obsession with an eternal hope. I *am* pursuing life on a whole new dimension. I *am* living courageously to be all that God has called me to be in Christ. My hope has changed my values, or rather, secured them even more deeply. I am a pilgrim on this journey. My ability to "be joyful in hope, patient in affliction, and faithful in prayer" is the force that pushes me forward, gets me out of bed, each day while I walk in the Midnight Hour.

Millions of people have gone before me in their experiences with the Midnight Hour. It isn't until long after I begin to use this name to describe my dark journey that I learn there are others who gave it similar names. St. John of the Cross referred to these days of dryness and estrangement from God as "the dark night of the soul." Henri Nouwen called them "the ministry of absence." The often quoted A. W. Tozer, "the ministry of the night."

In the book of Psalms, David beseeches God for answers for His seeming absence during his own dark night of the soul. God called David "a man after my own heart" and David was considered a close friend of God's, yet he cried out during his personal experience in the Midnight Hour:

Lord, why are you standing aloof and far away? Why do you hide when I need you the most? (Psalm 10:1 TLB)

My God, my God, why have you abandoned me? I have cried desperately for help, but still it does not come. (Psalm 22:1 GNT)

Why have you abandoned me? (Psalm 43:2 GNT)

This ministry of absence is a formidable time of plodding forward in the darkness, putting every bit of my faith in God to cast a glimmer of light and pierce through the darkness. All I ask for is a glimmer, enough light to see where to place my next step. Even when I'm scared. Even when it's dark. Even when I'm cold and lonely and we aren't speaking to one another. Even when the silence is deafening. His unfailing love keeps me—even in the Midnight Hour.

The LORD has hidden himself from his people, but I trust him and place my hope in him. (Isaiah 8:17 GNT)

What is faith? When asked this question throughout my life, the definition from Hebrews 11:1 rolled mechanically off my tongue: "Now faith is the substance of things hoped for, the evidence of things not seen" (NKJV). This seems to me like a vague answer that requires another answer. How does that translate to my life?

Like many Christians, I've often used my faith for something that I can eventually see with my eyes. We loosely use the words from 2 Corinthians 5:7: "I am walking in faith." We believe something is going to happen, will come to be, even though we have no proof of it yet. We are basically still walking in faith for something that pertains to the physical world, such as a job opportunity, money needed, having another child, improved health, a car, a house. In essence, then, most times we can eventually *see* it.

Through my journey in the Midnight Hour, I experience the truth in this verse in a dimension I've never had to go before.

The Amplified Classic translation of Hebrews 11:1 says, "Now faith is the assurance (the confirmation, the title deed) of the things [we] hope for, being the proof of things [we] do not see *and* the conviction of their reality [faith perceiving as real fact what is not revealed to the senses]." Since Michael's death, my faith has boiled down to this essential truth. To get out of bed each day, to breathe, to live again, or even to desire a new life, I must now be assured of the things I hope for: one all-powerful God, a savior in Jesus Christ, a heaven, and a redemption plan. I must be assured of my hope that Michael is experiencing these things now. I must be assured of my hope that all God's children will be gathered together in heaven one day, we win this battle here on earth, and all things come together for good to those who love the Lord. These are all things that I cannot see. They are not of this physical world. They are not revealed to the five senses.

But now I have a conviction of their reality.

This conviction keeps me breathing. It propels me forward—in search of life, healing, and an open door. I can see neither the road below me nor the path before me. With hands reaching toward Jesus, I walk on water in my storm with an unsinkable faith. A faith that surprises even me—but it is all I know to do. My feet miraculously land on steady ground with each baby step I take.

What I need is not of this world—and so I'm forced to walk in faith, believing God's word is true. I walk in faith that He is everything He says He is. I walk in faith that He is there, surrounding me with His presence, whether I see Him or not—whether I hear Him or not. I become sure of what I hope for and certain of what I don't see while traveling in the Midnight Hour.

Oftentimes since Michael's death, I sit down to write about my prevalent feelings, only to realize I've written about them previously. I'm amazed how these boomerang emotions circle back to me, or sometimes simply hover overhead and never go away at all. They are nearby, ready to lower on me at any given moment.

The recognition of the difficulty of walking through the Midnight Hour circles back continually. Today feels exactly like Day 62—many months ago. But now it's Day 211, and the Midnight Hour remains all around.

DAY 211

It continues to be hard—all of it—as I sort out everything, heal from the wound, and learn a new way of living. It requires things of me that I have never had to do before. The first few months were hard because they were consumed with the excruciating pain of the sudden loss of Michael. I missed him more than I ever could have imagined. But during those first few months, my life coasted for a while on auto-pilot. ("My life" meaning everything it takes to run a household and to be a single parent.) It continues to be just as hard, but now it's more than just missing Michael.

At first I was only dealing with a broken heart, but now I also feel scared of the future with every step I take. I'm apprehensive, plus I am carrying around my healing heart. Now I'm struggling every day with my "new normal" life.

Imagine this . . .

When you are young and you get married, or even don't, you establish a plan for your life. You begin your journey in the direction you feel will take you to your destination. You have a mental image of how you want your life to look in the future. Each day you walk out that plan, that dream, that vision, on the road that lies before you.

You have a map, and you feel like you can and are reading it correctly. Life has a rhythm to it . . . It feels safe.

Then one day, the road suddenly turns pitch black. Your travel companion is mysteriously snatched away. You are now alone, shuffling your feet, trying to determine where he, or she, went, and the direction you must now go. It's as if you have been picked up and transplanted to another country where all of the rules have changed, even which side of the road to drive on. The physical map has been destroyed. You must rely on your memory, and your instincts, for the details on the direction of your journey. You keep asking yourself, "Now, why was I going in this direction? Can the celebration of arriving at my destination feel the same without my original travel companion? Did I reach that destination and now there is a new one? Or has everything changed, not just the road but everything that propels me toward the destination?"

I must face these questions and truly meditate on the answers. I could turn away from facing these questions or problems, as many people do, and move on pretending my journey is the same but with one less person, only this would be pretending—a way of numbing reality. I would not learn from it or become wiser for it. There are no shortcuts on this journey. People have tried shortcuts, but their wound only shows up later in life because it didn't heal properly. It is a journey we must take slowly, seeing and feeling everything along the way.

It makes me think of a blind person learning how to "see" a new way. Their senses of smell, touch, and hearing are heightened to help them experience life more fully. If they refuse to learn the new ways, they will continue to bump into things and live a frustrated life. They must learn to navigate with a new map.

People have said there is no right or wrong way to grieve. This is truth, but only partial truth. I also believe there is a healthy, productive way to grieve and an unhealthy, deceiving-yourself way to do it. Everyone grieves differently, but I think it has to be better for us, in the long run of life, to face it, question it, learn from it, feel it, and embrace all that we can in order for it to help us, not hinder us, in the rest of our walk here on this earth. The way we do all those things can look differently, but I think we must do them in some way, shape, or form.

I have to trust God in a very real way. I have no choice but to trust Him during this dark journey. I must lean on Him. I'm reminded of a verse that I have prayed for years, Proverbs 4:25: "Let your eyes look straight ahead, and your eyelids look right before you" (NKJV). And also Psalm 119:105: "Your word is a lamp to my feet and a light to my path" (NKJV). Without God as my guide, there would be no light on this new road. A lamp only shows the light directly at your feet and maybe one step ahead, but at least it is some light.

This is all I can see: directly at my feet and one step ahead. It's scary, but there's also a glimmer of light way down the path—like at the end of a very long tunnel—but it's only the size of a speck right now. The road may zigzag all over the place, but that I cannot see, and it's probably best that way. At least the light is there. I am walking the road with apprehension and uncertainty, and am wounded…but at least I am walking. I am walking with my eyes wide open, facing every twist and turn with an unaware boldness.

CHAPTER 5

In the Land of the Living

Let my soul be at rest again, for the LORD has been good to me. He has saved me from death, my eyes from tears, my feet from stumbling. And so I walk in the LORD's presence as I live here on earth [in the land of the living].

—PSALM 116:7–9 (NLT)

ALL OF HIS CLOTHES ARE just as he left them. I enter the closet, partially close the door, and turn to my right, as I have done countless times this year. I stare at all of his clothing. I run my hands down the arms of his suit coats. I take a deep breath, releasing some of the heaviness, and then give myself a moment. At this point, I usually turn back to my side of the closet, on the left.

Not tonight.

I'm experiencing a different kind of grieving today. I feel a huge, silent void in my activities. I can't put my finger on anything specific—it's an overall *I need him today.*

I touch his suit coats, but then, after a long, meditative

pause, I impulsively grab the shoulders of a bunch of dress shirts. Leaning over, I stick my nose into the collars. Slowly, deeply, I inhale. I want to breathe in any bit of his smell I can encounter. Surprisingly, it's there—all of it. I'm caught off guard. I choke and begin to cry: lament at its very core. The mixture of the smell of his skin and his cologne is just as it was when I hugged him after work each day. I lean my face back against his shirts, tears running onto the shoulders as I breathe him into my memory. I'm comforted, yet I feel even more vulnerable surrounded by his smell with his shirts against my face. I've heard of people who keep the clothing of their loved ones who have died. I get it now.

I cry for him. I cry to God for help. I know Michael is in heaven—an amazing place. This settles my heart enough to make it somewhat bearable. He is in a better place than I. But God! In this master plan of life and death, couldn't You give us something a little more tangible when our loved ones die? Not solely hope and the knowledge of the everlasting life yet to come? Is the extreme separation necessary? Why are we allowed to love like this, only for it to be taken away without our knowing when it will be restored? I've always been able to handle the knowledge of the spiritual realm, but now that someone I love is *in* that spiritual realm, it's hard to bear the separation between the two worlds.

Tears in the closet. Life contemplated in the closet. Alone in the closet.

I emerge from the closet feeling spent but also as if more weight has lifted off my chest.

I don't know what it is about our closet, but I continue having meltdowns in this stark-white, small space. When we remodeled our house in 2000, we added a second story above the new guest bedroom and the keeping room next to the kitchen. We relocated the master bedroom to the new wing. Michael designed and installed our closet-organization system, and I whitewashed the hardwood floors on my hands and knees. So maybe I have more meltdowns here because it is a space we created together. Maybe it's because it feels soundproof once the door is partially closed or because the presence of his clothing reminds me of his strength—which reminds me of what it feels like to be protected by him.

Maybe it's because the closet is such a quiet, private place, a personal space. Michael and I grabbed conversations there as we got ready for church and date nights or changed clothes at the end of a day. It's very tight quarters. One of us in the closet at a time—or possibly both, but only if he went in first with me closely on his tails. (Then we had to scoot over to his side of the closet and shut the door.) We had an established necessary choreography whenever we got ready at the same time. We stepped in and out of the closet to ask an opinion on what we chose to wear. We filled each other in on what happened in our worlds that day. We often decompressed with a glass of wine as we chatted and waltzed in and out of the closet.

Getting ready for our dates was probably our favorite part of the date, most likely because we had each other's undivided attention. Oftentimes Michael came home from work on a

Thursday night to find me changing in the closet for our date. I cracked the door open while peeking my head out to find him standing there with two glasses of wine. "Hello!" he'd say with a big smile, then give me a kiss as he handed me a glass. He paced the floor outside the closet and talked to me while I continued dressing. I emerged fully dressed, then touched up my makeup as I talked to him while he changed his clothes. The date drink was always shared in the bathroom area or closet. Sometimes when he came home he caught me already dressed and standing in front of the mirror freshening up. He entered with our wine, saying, "Well, don't you look nice!"

I kept my side of the closet fairly neat, but his side of the floor was typically scattered with shoes he had worn and not returned to their shelves. Without saying anything, I periodically put all of the shoehorns back into his dress shoes and placed them neatly on the shelves. The shelf with his lounging pants got messy, too. Occasionally, I folded and stacked them back into order. At night, during his turn in the closet, he popped his head out and around the door. "The closet looks great! Thanks, babe!"

My closet has remained a personal place this year since his death, but in a different way. It's God and I—and my memories of Michael. In Michael's absence, the closet is a lonely place. Because of that, I allow myself to make a big mess in there. I thought if I stood in a clean closet with lots of floor space, I would feel his absence even more. My shoes have formed huge piles all over the floor. Getting dressed is not the same. I no longer have his opinion of the perfect outfit. I wore what he liked—I enjoyed it that way. I felt prettier knowing it was something that pleased him. Besides, he had great taste. When I couldn't make up my mind about what to wear, deferring to his opinion was my usual backup plan.

I often think about purging and restoring order back to my side of the closet; maybe it will feel better that way. But then again, it may not. It might give the illusion that all is back to normal—whatever that "new normal" everyone keeps mentioning is. No matter what the closet looks like, even if I have to sit amid a mountain of shoes, it's one of the safe places I go to grieve "inside the box."

My children and I are often on different tracks of the grieving process. Sometimes there are two of us inside the box, while two are outside the box; one inside the box crying, one inside the box watching a movie alone, one wanting to talk, one wanting to be silent, one wanting to be happy and move on, one wanting to fall back. It's a continual forward-and-back motion. But after observing the differences in how we approach our grief, I also discover a commonality. We all need time both inside and outside of what I've come to think of as "the grief box." Inside the box is where we go to handle our deep pain, our thoughts, and our tears in private. It is inside that box that we absorb most of the shock from each wave of grief. And yet, being inside the box also exposes the children and me to the great pain of our grief. We can't stay in that place twenty-four hours a day. We *have* to come outside for air—give ourselves permission to set down the pain. Outside of the box is where we attempt to live our "normal" lives, in the land of the living. We go outside to survive. We go inside to survive. We cope with our grief in both places.

There is not a right way to do this. We all come up for air at different times and for different durations. Our needs, ages, maturity, thoughts, and fears are all vastly different from one another's. Without being told a magic formula, my children naturally open and close their boxes. They swim up for air, as they need the sun to shine on their faces. Their preferred ways of coping began to show up immediately, but the unique choices they make to suit their individual needs became quite clear as early as the evening of Michael's visitation.

With over two thousand people to greet at the visitation, the wait time to see the family was over two hours. After three hours of standing in one place while receiving people, it was decided things would move along faster if I moved down the line instead of guests walking toward us. At Belhaven University's Performing Arts Center, the line came up to the front doors from the sidewalk down the street, through the right side of the foyer, down the right side of the auditorium, across the stage where the live band played soft music and Michael's casket stood, down the steps to the left of the stage, up the left side of the auditorium, and then finally to the family standing in the left side of the foyer. The family split up in order for us to see all of the guests.

Michael Anthony went to the room where dinner was served to eat and socialize. It was lively with many older teenagers and young adults from our church. He stayed outside the box the entire evening. I never saw him again until it was time to go. Mia did her own, adult-like greetings throughout the auditorium, in her quiet, sincere, and compassionate way. Her mood seemed to straddle inside and outside the box.

(I was extremely moved by and in awe of her strength.) I moved down the line with Nanette following along behind me for support and meeting any needs I had. Julia chose a completely different way to handle the change of plans than her siblings.

While shaking hands in introductions, hugging people, and receiving condolences, I suddenly became aware that my Velcro Girl was quietly moving along right beside me. My heart was moved. She patiently met every person there, holding my hand or my elbow as we walked together through the staggering number of people. Her presence inadvertently comforted me, even though she was at my side because of the comfort it brought her. She remained there the rest of the evening—unknowingly coping inside her box amid thousands of people.

Being overly extroverted, Michael Anthony needs more air than the rest of us. By nature, he's always been a highly active and social child. He never meets a stranger. He played tackle football from the ages of six to twelve. Because of his size, we weren't overly concerned about an injury; he was always taller and stronger than anyone else on the field. At the time of Michael's death, he was five foot seven and weighed 175—not too small for a twelve-year-old. Except for the one year he played center, he always played defensive tackle. All season, every single year, his father reminded him to hit his man. Instead, he typically pushed his man on the shoulders, even though he was clearly large enough to make lunch meat out of him. When asked why he didn't tackle the guy, his standard answer was "But Dad, he's my friend!" His dad's reply: "You just met him!" Michael Anthony would go on to explain that they talked in between plays and had things in common! After becoming fast friends, the two agreed not to take each other down. Michael resorted to paying him for each tackle and double payment for sacking the quarterback. This began to work!

During the first few months after Michael's death, Michael Anthony played lots of tennis; beat his drums; went turkey hunting, fishing, and camping; earned an Eagle Scout merit badge; played in the neighborhood creek; had horseback riding lessons; and worked on his target practice using ketchup bottles. It wears me out just typing everything he did outside the box—so different from his sisters and me! He also had some downtime with video games or dance-offs with his sisters while playing Just Dance on the Wii. There's nothing wrong with him doing these things. His personal makeup requires him to be active or on a specified schedule. Our schedule has been thrown out the window for a while—it's good for him to do things that are fun and provide a physical and social outlet.

When he opens his box to go inside, which isn't often, he prefers a private place, and mostly in my presence—and in my bedroom. At night, when it's just the two of us, his brain settles down and he likes having conversations with me as his mind slowly drifts to his life questions and feelings. (He still does this with me at age eighteen.) Sometimes he cries and simply says, "I miss Dad." One night he told me that some people who had been at our house made him feel like I was the only one experiencing the loss and pain. They implied he was supposed to be able to carry on his daily duties and responsibilities. Through his tears, he told me this wasn't fair to him;

I agreed. I shower him with hugs, squeezes, and kisses when he slows down enough to receive them. We pray together at night—and cry together. Because of his busyness and planning activities, it may appear to those looking on from the outside that he is not grieving. Oh, but he is. He simply cannot hold his breath as long as I can while inside the box.

Julia has a quiet strength. She cried her share of tears both publicly and privately in the first week. Like Michael Anthony, she loves to be around people but needs more time in quiet spaces as well. The first few days following Michael's death, we had hundreds of people pass through our home . . . literally. Wearing sweatpants and a sweatshirt, she parked her body in the bay window in our front sitting room, her pillow and favorite comfy blanket in tow. The location brought her comfort, as it allowed her to listen or visit with people, or she could simply stretch out, cover herself with the blanket, and take periodic catnaps when she felt the need to pull away—she flowed in and out of her box. While in bed at night, she sometimes read my blog or cried herself to sleep.

Julia has two levels in her box. One is the space just for her, alone in her room. Above that is the level where she experiences the pain through my tears and conversations, often touching base with me more frequently during the day than the other two. She seems to feel loved and safe in that place. (She stayed locked in at that level the evening of the visitation.) Like Michael Anthony, she comes up for air to be silly; play Just Dance; have coffee or shop with friends; play the piano, guitar, or bass guitar; clean; or even play with Emma Claire, my four-year-old niece. Doing these things doesn't mean she isn't heartbroken and grieving. She is coming outside the box to breathe easier for a moment—in the land of the living.

Julia's primary way of feeling love and comfort from me is through physical touch. With that need, she makes herself "available" to me for a hug and a kiss almost every time she passes through the room. When friends came over to visit with me those first few weeks after the funeral, Julia sat right next to us without saying a word. She listened intently, sometimes tucking her arm into mine, and interacting with only a nod or a grin when in agreement with the emotion of the conversation. If I began to cry, she looked at me with love and understanding in her eyes. It seemed to help her to see me cry and openly share my heart. I saw her trying to sort things out in her own heart and mind.

Mia is mature beyond her years and always has been. She quickly and easily shows emotions without any embarrassment. She has her father's heart and an overdose of empathy for people who are hurting. During our early days of grieving, she would walk into the room, let her eyes meet mine, and it was as if her eyes were saying, "I get it. I am with you. I understand." (She still does this with me.) She hugs without saying a word, but her spirit says it all. Her eyes quickly fill with tears when she recognizes mine flowing freely down my face. She comes to me and holds me until the tears subside.

As her father did, as well as her siblings, Mia also draws energy from being around people. She prefers one-on-one time and, like Julia and me, also needs some pull-away time. The great thing about Mia is that she recognizes when she needs to be with someone. She makes her choices and meets those needs. A few Sundays after Michael's funeral, she felt the need to be in the church service, a need for social time but an intimate social time, because our church was a second family to her. Since my dad was still in town, they attended together.

At Michael's memorial service, our fully robed, multi-ethnic church choir sang, "I Want to Say Thank You." The song brought about the presence of God and a spirit of worship that seemed to catch most people off guard, a supernatural moment in the midst of a tragic event. Sitting in church that Sunday morning with my dad was Mia's first time hearing the choir since that day. Everyone stood and the choir began to sing "Bow Down" (for which her father had always sung the lead). My dad told me she melted on the spot right into her seat. She cried her way through the song.

She was comforted while surrounded by her church family, and yet, at the same time, she was able to pull away into her box by sitting down to cry alone. By the time she came home, she was relieved, stronger, and greeted me with a hug and her sweet smile. She goes inside her box to her bedroom more frequently than Julia and Michael Anthony do. We both do. She and I know our limits inside or outside the box and can hold our breath longer in either place. When Mia is outside the box, she's with friends; working at J.Crew; playing her guitar, mandolin, or piano; playing Just Dance; or chilling out with whoever is around. I think she's found a healthy balance of life inside and outside the box.

It would not be fair to judge any of us on how differently we respond to the same experience. My kids are unique, healthy, loving children who loved their father with all of their hearts.

They laughed when he laughed, prayed when he prayed, loved when he loved. They all had a great relationship with him, spent time with him, and knew they were special to him in each and every way. They miss him and long for him whether they are inside or outside their boxes. They need love and compassion in both places.

DAY 36

I know it is only natural for people to look at someone and make a judgment call on how they are doing—they look nice...dressed sharp...nice hair...smile on their face...can converse about the details of dailiness—hey, they even answered "good" when I asked how they were doing.

Things are not always what they seem.

In everyone's lives, there are immeasurable amounts of emotions, life experiences, hurts, and fears going on at a sub-level. We all learn how to show the side we think people want to see. I never wanted to be a poser and work hard at being transparent, but I find that putting on a face at times has become my way, the kids' way, of surviving outside of the box. We often put the face forward that we know people would rather see. It seems to make people more comfortable to be around us if they think we are "fine" and "moving along."

But don't be fooled, because beneath that surface, we still have needs that require us to dive deeply inside the box—even when we act and appear in a way that is acceptable to everyone else.

We must go about our daily activities, have conversations about other topics, speak when spoken to, smile back to people, and even ask other people how they are doing. In spite of my outward appearance and actions, inwardly I feel as if my entire insides are on fire. It is such a strange sensation. Sometimes I feel a heavy weight pressing on all sides of my body. Breathing often feels shallow. Other times, while listening to someone talk to me, a consuming fire takes over my body and engulfs me up to my ears. The background noise tunes out. I feel as if I am in a soundproof room, and yet everyone is talking and carrying on with their conversations. Sometimes it is simply an ache or an empty feeling, while other times it's just plain painful.

If the kids and I laugh, the laughter is real, but when the laughter is over, the void, and the pain, are still there. If you look hard enough into our eyes, you can see it. I see it in their eyes. It's under there, but they are surviving—and so am I. We are walking against a strong tide or wind. It is a slow walk, but we are progressing, in spite of its force and the pain that blocks our vision at times and makes our eyes hurt.

I found some verses that speak directly to these thoughts. God continues to amaze me how he meets all of my needs by bringing very specific Scriptures to mind to help me make it through each step. These are very pointed:

He gives strength to the weary
and increases the power of the weak.
Even youths grow tired and weary,
and young men stumble and fall;
but those who hope in the LORD
will renew their strength.

They will soar on wings like eagles; they will run and not
grow weary,
they will walk and not be faint. (Isaiah 40:29–31 NIV)

*Lord, renew our strength. Will we ever run again? For now, let us
not faint.*

I love the LORD, for he has heard my voice;
he heard my cry for mercy.
Because he turned his ear to me,
I will call on him as long as I live.
The cords of death entangled me,
the anguish of the grave came over me;
I was overcome by distress and sorrow.
Then I called on the name of the LORD:
"LORD, save me!"
The LORD is gracious and righteous;
our God is full of compassion.
The LORD protects the unwary;
when I was brought low, he saved me.
Return to your rest, my soul,
for the LORD has been good to you.
For you, LORD, have delivered me from death,
my eyes from tears,
my feet from stumbling,
that I may walk before the LORD
in the land of the living. (Psalm 116:1–9 NIV)

I believe His word is true. He has heard my cry for mercy. He delivers us while we are inside the box, so that we may walk outside the box, in the land of the living.

As a newborn baby is totally dependent on his mother and can only survive if he draws milk from her every couple of hours for nourishment and strength, I have to draw near to God at close and regular intervals in order to have the strength to make it through each day. I am weak and fragile, totally dependent on my Heavenly Father to sustain me.

I am the main source of stability for my children. I gain physical, mental, and spiritual strength for my household in my box. Just as I lose strength if I stay outside of the box too long, my faith also quickly falters. Fear and doubt come crashing in: my heart pounds, my blood pressure shoots up and down, my concentration leaves me; sometimes simply breathing is difficult. I intentionally hang on to every shred of faith I have—and the only way I can do it is through frequent trips back to the box. Quiet and focused before God, my peace is restored. My body and mind receive a fresh new calm. There are no magic prayers or formulas or specific Scriptures, simply recognition that I need Him and depend on Him.

This simple act of acknowledging my need for Him shows I still have faith in Him. All hope is not lost. Even without the strength or the will to speak out loud to God, my silent cries of the heart to Him bolster my faith each time I go inside the box and sit silently in His presence. As Psalm 116 expresses, inside the box I am at rest again. God is still good to me. He's saving me from death and the pain of Michael's death, from my tears, and from stumbling in the fear that grips me. Because I am now at rest, I feel strong enough to walk with God in the land of the living, outside of the box.

Many people assumed that when I wasn't posting anything new on my blog, things must have been going well. Other people told me they began to pray even more for the children and me because they recognized it could've meant I was pulling away, going deeper inside the box. The latter was the truth. Even though I occasionally appeared as if I was functioning and doing my daily tasks, the longer I operated *outside the box*, the more I craved the solitude *inside the box*. Sometimes I had to function for long periods of time in the land of the living, when all I really wanted was to disappear to my room and tend to my aching heart. It was always present, no matter what I was doing or where I was. The busier life was with schedules and decision-making, or the longer I went without writing, the more lonely and sad I became. Desperate for time to myself, I had to pull away in the quiet, where I could write, reflect, and cry with no one watching—or do absolutely nothing.

Outside or inside the box—I'm pulled in both directions at all times. I get tired of being strong, tired of doing the necessary, tired of being the decision-maker, and tired of getting things done. I don't necessarily want to be weak; I'm only tired of being strong—outside the box. I found that writing on a daily basis is the best healing balm for me. Facing the reality through writing is much better for me than staying in a busy state, which doesn't allow me the time to feel, discern, or sit with God. There has to be a balance between the two, or my emotional state seems to suffer. Most all of the time, I only suffer if it's too much time outside the box.

In *Good Grief*, Granger Westberg explains, "People are off talking about other things and we are left alone with our sorrow. Everyone has forgotten our tragedy." This feels so true. It seems easier for others to move on with their lives—and quickly. It feels as if some even assume we're moving right along the same as they've done, but "we are left alone with our sorrow." Westberg goes on to say:

> The pace of modern life may have something to do with this. The minute people finish one event they are off to another and another...Most people do not take time to help work through another's losses. We also find, when we attempt to get back into life again, it is much too painful. We would rather grieve than fight the battle of coping with new situations. Grieving is painful, but not as painful as having to face entirely new decisions every hour. We are more comfortable in our grief than in the new unpredictable world.

Even though grieving, in and of itself, is difficult, it often proves to be more painful to face new decisions every hour. It's much easier to stay in a place where decisions can be avoided, but that isn't possible. It's a hard but good thing in the healing process to make new decisions. A good thing to face all the realities of Michael being gone. Life *has* to go on, even though it hurts. Decisions are hard and painful, no matter how big or small. It's exhausting to face them for long periods of time.

I find myself carrying more grief on the inside because I feel like people are tired of hearing about it, or seeing it. There's an unspoken projected feeling that they are ready to move on—and want me to do the same, back to business as usual. But I still need to talk about it. It's still all I feel. Westberg continues to say, "Our modern way of life makes it difficult for us to grieve about any loss in the presence of other people. We are forced to carry all of the grief within ourselves." Case in point: the need for me to go to my room to really let down. Westberg says:

This is particularly true in the loss of a loved one through death. When many of us were children, people grieved more openly. The men wore black armbands and the women wore black veils for six months to a year...so that everyone was reminded daily of their loss. But we somehow have the impression that grief is out of place in our society. We conduct a quiet conspiracy of silence against it. We try never to talk about grief, and certainly never display it by any outward sign. We offer our sympathy to our grieving friends immediately after their loss has occurred, but from then on we say in effect, "Now, let's get back to business as usual again."

After a friend of mine lost her father, she noticed people avoiding her and the subject of his death. It hurt her. She said, "People are missing out by not sharing in the grieving process.

It enriches the lives of both people." Death is as much a part of this life experience as life itself. We can learn as much from it as we can from life. It takes a long time to work through the fog, but when it slowly begins to lift, we see things differently. Why do people want to rush through it or push it down or away, as if it's not really there? This *is* life. We must deal with death, grow in wisdom and compassion through it with our friends as they walk through their loss.

Grieving—it's a long road. I want to say to my friends and family, please hang in there with us. Allow us to take our time, handle us with care, hug us, listen to us—not too much advice—love, pray often; join us when we stop to rest as we remember this great man and recognize what a deep loss we are experiencing in this life. We are still on this journey and it hurts, whether we are inside or outside the box.

CHAPTER 6

Strength Waning

No discipline seems pleasant at the time, but painful.
Later on, however, it produces a harvest of
righteousness and peace for those who have been
trained by it.

—Hebrews 12:11 (niv)

Piles of paperwork as a result of Michael's death seem never-ending. If I don't stay on top of it daily, it overwhelms me—I'm fooling myself. I'm overwhelmed even when I stay on top of it. If I go out of town, I try to forget about it, but it's there, waiting for me when I return, like an endless pile of physical burdens. Burdens I never asked to carry or even feel qualified to address. I'm thankful I have people in place to help me handle all of my questions.

Today I wake up with a mission: I'm going to conquer the entire pile of paperwork. A pile that now fills one-half of my breakfast table, even though I work on it daily. There are papers to file, piles of business papers with questions for certain people like attorneys, accountants, bankers, and financial planners, as well as powers of attorney. Then there are the questions for my friend Amy, who teaches me how to do my entire bookkeeping system. Before having children, she worked in wealth management at a bank and presently keeps the books for her husband's business, as well as for their household. Amy shares with me what she has—a gift for balancing bank accounts and setting up budgets. She makes it look so easy that this has become one area that no longer feels quite so burdensome.

There are piles of Michael's business mail to open, more thank-you notes to write for donations, papers to read, personal notes to read that continue to arrive in the mail, papers to sign, bills to pay, and paperwork that is simply awaiting a decision. I make my three-page to-do list, delegate to my sister Julie what she can do without me, and then begin to conquer my pile of burdens—and it's only seven thirty in the morning.

I need sleep.

I'm focused and determined. I feel imaginary blinders helping me focus on each item without any thoughts or emotions. This is "business"—and God is covering me with grace to treat it this way. I face the facts with a levelheaded mind in order to stay in motion. I make great progress, so I switch to sorting through a pile of papers with Michael memorabilia. My aunt Jerri put together a scrapbook for me from a folder I had kept over the years. There were countless articles from newspapers and magazines, as well as the magazine covers, all with stories of Michael. The articles covered his music or his architecture, or featured him as the Renaissance man he was. I gave her the folder on February 24, and she had the book completed by the visitation the next night, on the twenty-fifth. I have left the scrapbook out in my sitting room for us to peruse anytime we feel like it. Guests like looking at it, too.

I get up from the table and go to the sitting room to slip a piece of memorabilia into the back of the scrapbook. I reach down, lift all of the pages to the back in one turn, and catch a glimpse of one of my favorite pictures of Michael smiling back at me. The imaginary blinders drop. It's a cute picture, the look he gave me when he was up to something, like a surprise, or when he was amused with himself. As I look at his face, I hear him say, "Well, hey there!" He often said this when he came upon me by surprise in our bedroom or closet—and thought I was looking especially beautiful. He said it if I showed up at his office unannounced, as if I was a sight for sore eyes.

I stand still and slow down enough to peer again at his face over the edge of the pages that my hand is holding. Tears fill my eyes. Instinctively, I hear myself speak out loud to him. "I miss you." I smile back at him through the blurring tears. The room is silent. I hold my gaze with his for a few moments.

Back to the kitchen table—the tears are now everywhere I turn. *Keep pressing through it, Jené.* On the table is a letter I just received from Michael Anthony from camp. He said he is "working through this homesickness." I understand what he means. I'm working through this homesickness, too. I am homesick for our home when Michael was in it.

I continue working on the piles. Distracted and flustered, I crumble. I lose my direction, as well as my ability to approach all this as business or as a simple task to check off my list. Taking a deep breath, I step back. It's time to seek refuge inside my box.

Sitting on the corner of my bed, I stare at the wall in front of me. I realize there is no place to get away from it. He is everywhere. I sob as everything staring back at me is a memory of him. The black-and-white family photo taken in front of the Sistine Chapel in Rome is hanging on the wall. Next to it, a beautiful mirror made from old architectural materials he chose on one of his shopping outings. On top of the lingerie chest, sitting underneath the mirror, stands one of my favorite pictures of us with Nanette and Peter. It was taken on Peter's surprise fortieth birthday weekend in Texas—we are all squeezing one another in a big bear hug. Next to the picture is a square glass vase holding all of the shells Michael and I gathered on our walks together at Rosemary Beach. Then there is the huge glass urn that holds all of the rose petals from the dozen roses he gave me with the birth of each child: red for Mia's birth, pink for Julia's, and yellow for Michael Anthony's. My eyes continue crying as they move slowly from one object to the next, to the next, remembering each moment they represent.

Keep breathing, Jené.

My drenched face now spills tears off my chin to my lap.

My eyes land on the elephant sitting in the room. Slouching and plopped on the floor near the ottoman sits his stylish, Italian leather satchel—exactly where I placed it on February 23 after it was retrieved from his car. On top of the ottoman is his leather notebook. He bought it in Florence during our last visit to Italy. He loved the smell of good leather. I spot his glasses sitting on top of the leather notebook—his trendy, frameless, signature glasses that are now bent and missing the glass on the left side. In a crazy, impulsive second, I think about putting them on; I quickly dismiss the thought. I decide to open his leather notebook and read some notes.

I gingerly open it, and the smell of the leather rises to my nose. I cry even more because it smells just as he liked it to smell. I touch everything carefully because it's still covered in glass dust from the accident, now over six months ago. It would have been sitting on the front seat of his car at the time of the wreck. I slowly read through all of his business notes that had been taken since January. Notes from every meeting he attended. I find notes taken on Valentine's Day and notes taken from a meeting with his partners on February 21—and 22. I see a sheet of paper with something handwritten all over it folded in a side pocket. I open it and begin to cry yet a little harder. It's a prayer he wrote for the grand opening of a fire station he designed for the city of Flowood in Mississippi. He had been asked to say the prayer:

Father, we stand before You today humbled by what You have done. We're so thankful for this day that we celebrate Your handiwork once again in the city of Flowood. In a world with so much uncertainty, we're grateful for the vision and commitment of the city leaders and firefighters who constantly lean on Your certainty for guidance. Let this facility remind us of their persistent dedication to the citizens of Flowood, who, above all, they recognize as being Your people. We ask You protect the lives of those that will use this facility and as they go out, that they would return safely. We thank You that this facility was not built in vain, but to Your glory by a city that honors You.

Now we ask You to bless this fellowship, as we honor what You have done.

In Jesus' name I pray, Amen.

Time's up, Jené. Get back outside the box.

I fold up the prayer, then slowly tuck it back into the pocket of the leather notebook. I sit still on the corner of my bed for a while, attempting to "get it together." Allowing the tears and the breathing to slow down, I wipe my face with the crook of my arm. My eyes scan one last time over the wave train that just struck me. *Inhale.* I choose to stand and make my descent outside the box, to return to the pile of burdens that awaits me.

I feel my strength waning with each day, each week, that goes by. Huge draws are made on my strength every single moment. I take care of the necessary, but at times I push myself too much. While in the moment, I think to myself, *I can do this. It's just a task. Keep going a little farther. Keep a level head. Make your decisions clear. Keep moving.* It always hits me later when I'm in a place to let down my guard. Like in the familiar closet.

The children and I go to Michael's office building for the first time since his death. It's the beginning of a week that finally brings my strength to a temporary halt. It's necessary to go to the office building because I'm selling it. He'd been in this location for eleven years. He turned it into a place where creative minds produced great architecture; a Barranco Architecture subculture existed. We walk in, and it looks as if they all had just stepped out for lunch. It's messy. Drawings lie everywhere. Coffee is still in the pot. Dirty mugs are in the sink. A note Mia wrote to him on his marker board is still there.

The kids and I wander around the place with our own personal agendas. Julia wants to be sure we bring home his coffee mugs. Michael Anthony wants to explore all of his favorite spots—like the drawer where one of Michael's employees stashed snacks and always gave him anything he wanted when he came to play in the office. Mia's agenda is similar to mine: absorb and reflect. We look, discover, and feel his absence in this perfect little building on North State Street, his second home for so long.

I look all around each area, remembering who sat where and where we bought each piece of furniture, and stare at all of the watercolor renderings of projects lining the walls of the conference room, projects I remember discussing with him around our dining room table. I see all of the boxes in which we had placed his entire collection of architecture books just two weeks before he died. We were going to move them to his new office at the firm he was merging with. The day we packed them, we took only about eight of the thirty to forty boxes of books to the new office. He wanted time to figure out his new space before he brought the rest of the books.

The rest never made it to the new office. I hold myself together for the sake of the children. They are focused on exploring.

I carry home some family photos Michael had placed in a box to take to his new desk. One is a picture of Michael Anthony dressed in a Civil War uniform I had sewn for him. He was pretending to sit on our dog like a horse, while doing his imitation of the salute by the crazy major in *Dances with Wolves*. The picture made Michael laugh every time he saw it. I had it framed for his office to help lighten up any heavy days. Another picture had been a Father's Day gift I gave him years ago. It holds three individual pictures of each child that I took while we were living in France for six weeks. Below the pictures, I placed a quote: "Priorities…A hundred years from now it will not matter what my bank account was, the sort of house I lived in, or the kind of car I drove…but the world may be different because I was important in the life of a child." Tucked in the corner of the frame was one of Michael's business-logo note cards. Written in his handwriting was his all-time favorite Scripture: "No discipline seems pleasant at the time, but painful. Later on, however, it produces a harvest of righteousness and peace for those who have been trained by it" (Heb. 12:11 NIV).

This verse is engraved on the bronze plate attached at the base of the granite bench bearing his name near his grave. He lived by this verse, and how appropriate it is that, in his own handwriting, on his Barranco Architecture stationery, it stayed before him daily, tucked into the corner of this framed picture of our children. Discipline of parenting, discipline of work, and discipline of the spirit. It's what he lived by.

The day after the office visit, I have a meeting with my estate attorney for the task of updating my will and testament and other business matters, not easy discussions to have. We are on the fourteenth floor in a corner meeting room with windows everywhere and a fabulous view—fabulous for everyone except me. I approach the view differently because I see many buildings Michael's architecture firm had designed, along with the cemetery where his body lies in the distance. I'm distracted and distant as I stare out the window watching the activity around the buildings that carry his thumbprint. In the distance is the new workout facility, The Club, whose grand opening is next month. Closer to me is the new Metropolitan Bank, whose metal framework is standing strong, ready for the addition of walls and interior spaces. (The same building for which he receives a design award posthumously many months later.) Over to my right is the lake belonging to the funeral home. I can hardly breathe as I see his touch on everything within view, but I must carry on with the meeting.

The day after my meeting on the fourteenth floor with the view, I have an appointment with Doug Dale, Michael's new partner in the firm with whom he had just merged. I scheduled some time with him to talk about everything from our feelings about Michael and grieving the loss of a spouse (he had lost his wife to cancer several years before), to what projects were going on and how the firm was doing. I also went there to gather up Michael's personal belongings, including the books we had packed and moved there.

I have no idea why I crammed all these experiences into one week.

I remind myself of Michael's favorite verse: "No discipline seems pleasant at the time, but rather painful. Later on, however, it produces a harvest of righteousness and peace...." These tasks require sheer discipline on my part. Discipline of mind, heart, and body.

All of his books are on the shelves above the desk, just as we placed them that Saturday in early February. When I walk into his office and see his books, it's like seeing old friends for the first time in years. These books represent his passion. So many of these reference books I have seen on the shelves our entire years of marriage. I pull one off the shelf called *The History of Architecture*, just so I can touch it and see his signature, a great signature. I cry over the book. After returning from the office building visit with the children a couple days ago, Mia asked me, "Mom, do we have his signature somewhere? I would really like to have it." I reassured her we had it in many places. I think of her as I look at his signature with the Barranco name sprawling out to a straight line with a dot at the end.

It's time to load up Michael's things. Julie arrives to help. In the silence, I begin putting his books in the boxes—it seems as if I just did it the previous week. Julie and I put everything on some dollies and are ready to head to the car when I remember the drawers.

I open up the top drawer, and for some reason there sits the receipt for the diamond earrings he gave me for Christmas the previous year. He'd purchased them on Christmas Eve as the icing on the cake to a wonderful Christmas. I had previously been told by the salesclerk at the jewelry store that he had come by to look at a pair, then decided to do some other last-minute shopping while he thought about it. He returned to purchase the earrings and also chose a larger size because, he said, "She deserves it." Michael told her it had been a tough year and I had stood by him, and the upcoming year was going to be better. Of all of the places for that receipt to be, here it is, sitting in this deserted drawer, waiting for me to find it. I pick it up and feel his heart. I slip it into my purse, then turn and notice a framed award on the wall that needs to go with me. It's honoring him as a past president of the Mississippi American Institute of Architects. Julie takes it off the wall, and we walk out together.

I don't want to talk on the drive home. I feel completely depressed. Weight has settled on my chest. My breathing is shallow. My stare is blank. Michael, you are really gone, aren't you? Such a void is left where your life once took up so much space. My heart aches for your presence. Another step of reality settles into my mind. I could sit in silence for hours, but we pass a building Michael had once claimed as his favorite building in Jackson, the War Memorial Building, next to the Old Capitol. I point it out to Julie. It was his favorite because it is a perfect example of classical architecture. I go back to my silence.

By the time I get ready for bed, I'm emotionally spent. All strength is gone. The week has taken its toll. I speak to God in my thoughts: *I feel my strength waning. My stores are spent. Lord, I need you. I can't do this alone.* I put on my pajamas in my closet—and then peek over at Michael's dress shirts still hanging on the other side of the closet. I'm desperate. Back to his shirts, I take a deep breath and breathe in all of his smells. It's like being wrapped in a blanket. I feel the backs of the shirts, touching the smoothly starched fabric I always felt on his back when I hugged him. It lasts only a few seconds but feels longer.

I hear Julia call for me to say good night as she approaches the closet. I come around the closet door with tears running down my face. She says, "I came to say good night." We stand there in an embrace for a long time. My crying continues as we stand silently in the doorway to my closet. She allows me to hold her as long as I need. I whisper, "I was smelling his shirts." I know she understands, she of all people. She is a smeller and always has been. She knows people by their smells and wanted Michael's pillow for the smell. She still sleeps with it.

I cry my way through washing my face and brushing my teeth. I look at myself in the mirror and see the pain in my face. There was some closure this week. Closure of the dream of his merger with Doug Dale, whom he admired and respected and had looked forward to working alongside. Closure of his relationships with his past employees. Closure of future possibilities for his creative ideas. Closure of a season.

After seven months and twenty-two days of fretful nights or not sleeping at all, I finally begin sleeping with a little more regularity. Anytime my body stops to rest, my mind is flooded with inner turmoil, the replaying of events of the week Michael died, or replaying our memories together.

I look forward to bedtime each night because it's the end of another day. I think to myself, *I made it through today*. A day of trials, hard decisions, parenting alone, living without Michael, missing him, and going through the motions of living. I feel that the end of each day brings me one day closer to the end of the Midnight

Hour. But then I dread the next part of the twenty-four-hour day because with it comes its own set of obstacles to overcome: sleep.

At night, I'm alone in my thoughts and feelings. The rest of the world is quiet, but during the past months my mind has been in a full state of motion. My state of "aloneness" is more pronounced in the dark hours of the night. The dark hours of the night are when I received visitors knocking on my door and learned about Michael's death. In the dark hours of the night my mind races through the trauma of the whole situation. Sleep comes in short spurts followed by suddenly awakening with a startle—then a couple of hours later, I fall into another short spurt of sleep. The cycle continues. I go to the bathroom throughout the night and get drinks of water just to give me something to do. I had forgotten what it felt like to fall asleep with ease, to sleep peacefully, or to feel any sort of rest.

When I wake up in the morning, I have a similar thought to the one I have at the close of each day: *I made it through another night.* I feel tormented for twenty-four-hour periods without any downtime to shut off my thoughts and emotions.

I went to a women's retreat in Colorado given by Ransomed Heart Ministries and John and Stasi Eldredge. It is upon returning from this retreat that my sleep and rest return back to me. Several women prayed over me while I was there, and I don't mean "Dear Lord, please be with Jené while she sleeps and help her walk through this time." These women prayed down heaven. They fought spiritual warfare on my behalf—targeted specific battles I was encountering around the clock. I felt different with each passing hour of the retreat. After two nights back at home, my body began to rest.

I begin feeling sleepy after I get in bed each night. Sometimes I fall asleep within thirty minutes and make it through the night without getting up. Sometimes I sleep hard. Sometimes I wake up in the morning and feel as if I have been in the deepest sleep I have ever known. (The sleep continues to be unpredictable several years later.) I'm not rested yet because I'm so far behind on it. Who knows how long it will be before true rest completely returns.

With a little rest for my body, I finally feel a slight upswing in the horizon. The elephant lifts off of my chest. I breathe again. I journeyed through what was possibly the most frightening part of the Midnight Hour. I will fear no evil, for He is with me. Dear God, this is hard! The angst, the moaning, the pouring of tears that have flooded my bed, the gut-wrenching pain; asking why or trying to understand does not bring peace. I acknowledge again that understanding is overrated. I simply trust God, move forward, and know He is there for me. I may gain understanding later, after we come out of this—but then again, I may not. Asking God for comfort and His presence, while staying alert to the enemy's attacks that come in the valley, is the only way to pull through the battle. There is a battle; this is a battle. It is dark and it is taking every bit of my strength, but I finally witness some small victories, like sleep.

I lay down and slept,
yet I woke up in safety,
for the LORD was watching over me. (Psalm 3:5 NLT)

CHAPTER 7 ∽

Married, Single, Divorced, Widowed

What allows one to hurt so much is the ability to love
so powerfully.

—PETER ROBINSON COFFIN

> ...With this ring, I thee wed, to have and to hold, from
> this day forward...'til death do us part.

I LOOK DOWN AT MY WEDDING RING—the ring that has been on my finger for twenty-five years now. It's still there, after more than half a year of my being a widow. I'm in a quandary. So what now? Just take it off and put it in my jewelry drawer? This ring, which I have never taken off except when mixing raw ground meat with my hands? This ring, which made me feel protected? This ring, which made me feel loved and honored? This ring, which stood for my steadfast commitment and fidelity "'til death do us part"? This ring, which I spin around with my thumb on cold days? This ring, which symbolized to me all it was meant to symbolize?

This step is a tough one for me, a first step I am dragging my feet toward. Removing this symbol of my covenant with

Michael is much harder than simply slipping a ring off of my finger. I love our set of rings. They are so "us." He chose Italian gold, of course, eighteen-karat gold instead of fourteen, with texture and design, not simply smooth bands with a diamond solitaire sitting on top.

When I was told about Michael's accident, I didn't want to believe it was him in that car who had died, until they brought me back his wedding ring and his Italian gold crucifix necklace—both of which he never took off. Then I would know.

They hang around my neck now.

I know there are all kinds of options I can choose for my ring, like wearing it on my right hand and putting a different ring on my wedding finger, or making it into a necklace in some creative way, but then it becomes a new symbol altogether, a symbol of the past, something that used to be, something to be remembered—not something to live by daily. But it could also become a symbol of hope in all things good. It was a good marriage, a solid marriage, a marriage based on godly principles, a marriage that defied the mainstream and did not become a statistic. It was a marriage that stood for something. But if I wear my ring daily, won't it be even more difficult to move forward? There will never be the perfect time to remove it from my finger. One day soon I probably just need to do it, without putting any more thought into it—dive in and get it over with, rip off the Band-Aid.

I tried this method last week when it was time to pick figs from our trees in the backyard. Michael ordered and planted the trees because he loved figs. It was a nod to his Italian heritage and his childhood memories of his Papaw. Michael did the picking of the figs during harvest season. He would pop a few into his mouth on his way back to the kitchen, then comment on their beauty and perfection as he came through the french door. I decided last week to grab a bowl and march straight outside to gather all of the bright, purplish fruit from the tree. No pomp and circumstance—just go do it. With every fig I removed from the tree, I affirmed to myself, "I can do this. I can do this." It didn't really work. Tears filled the rims of my eyes. There was no joy or beauty in the moment, as there always was when Michael picked them. Making the fig tarts won't be the same without Michael drooling over their beauty and flavor.

So much for the idea of just sucking it up and doing it.

No, I think I need to remove my ring in a calm moment of solitude in my bedroom. I'll probably remove it, admire it, remember his proposal, kiss it, and put it safely in the original ring box. With this ring, we became one—for better, for worse, for richer, for poorer, in sickness and in health. 'Til death do us part.

I'm frequently alone in the evenings this summer. The kids are fully engaged in their lives outside the box. Of course, they don't realize that these activities keep their anxieties in check, but that's exactly what they do.

Mia works at J.Crew and the dance studio where she takes hip-hop classes. She's excited about her upcoming freshman year in college, which has its own built-in distractions and events. It keeps her eyes on the future. Julia has swim practice every day, plus multiple swim meets. There are social outings with her team members, plus her running endeavors, and frequent dates with friends and mentors over coffee at Starbucks. Michael Anthony swims on the summer league team, plays tennis as much as possible, rides his bike long distances, and spends countless hours with friends.

Their musical talents still prove to be a healthy outlet for them. Music training hasn't missed a beat this year. I think it's because they enjoy the relationships they have with each teacher. The girls even joined in with a string group consisting mostly of adults. They perform at the CelticFest and other venues. I feel they love the practice time with the group more than anything. It's become a second family to them. The drums are an obvious energy release for Michael Anthony. He unknowingly uses drumming as an inside-the-box experience. He puts on his headphones and plays along to all kinds of genres—stepping into his own world while he plays, leaving all of his thoughts behind.

The house feels big and I feel lonely. Since the kids are out, it's painfully quiet.

It's another evening alone in the house. As usual, I miss my evening chat time with Michael. I step outside to walk Brady— I feel the sadness and tears creep up on me, but I don't want to go there. Sometimes I have little conversations with God while I walk Brady—mostly short pleas for help. Tonight I choose to stay outside the box. My cell phone is in my pocket. I call Julie for a distraction. "I feel a moment coming on me and I'm trying to stop it—so I called you. Talk to me about anything. I don't want to talk about how I am doing." We talk about her plans for the next few months as I walk my dog around the neighborhood. With determination, I push through the moment. I walk back in the house and eat dinner by myself. Even in these silent evenings, I feel God's presence fill every inch of the air.

I always enjoyed solitude. Sometimes I'm probably a borderline recluse. In the past, I enjoyed exercising alone, driving alone, or sitting alone in a quiet house. I never required much girlfriend time or recreation time. Michael and I were very independent of other people while dependent on each other. Even in that, we had a strong, healthy independence within our marriage. Michael was more of an extrovert. I was content with very few social outings. I liked my simple life—but the solitude is not the same now.

To me, solitude has a positive connotation to it. Solitude is something we strive to fit somewhere into our busy lifestyles. It is something that recharges us, enlarges our minds, gives us time to catch our breath and even see things with a new perspective. This seems to have reversed on me lately. It's not solitude, but more like loneliness. I need more socializing than I have ever needed in my life. I have several friends who make themselves available for all of the little visits required to help me make it through the days. I still need between two to three hours a day of true solitude. Any time alone beyond that takes a lonely turn. This is when I look to family and friends to fill the void. It may be a phone call, a visit with a neighbor, or even a quick trip in the car to get coffee from Starbucks. All of these things work for me.

It's more difficult to solve the lonely spells in the evenings than in the daytime. Like many people, I want to unwind at night—maybe move in and out of some easy conversations or simply do things silently among and around people. These are comforting acts. Lonely evenings like tonight teach me more about my new normal. I change and reinvent my evenings in an attempt to keep the loneliness at bay. It's a slow evolution—a process of trial and error, a struggle for balance. In the past, I felt balanced for the most part, but as I spend my evenings alone now, I feel the weights shift as I figure out which areas need more, like socializing, and which areas need less, like spending time in solitude.

Life itself pulls me more and more outside the box lately. I think of life like a river. A river knows where to go. My life knows where to go, and it's taking me there—and the current carries me outside the box. It knows what I need. The children and I are moving along together, as we have to, but in fundamental ways, alone—alone because every grieving person must grapple for guidance for his or her own journey through deep waters, trusting the river.

I had never fully realized how closely intertwined my days were with Michael's until he was gone. I feel alone and insecure—I don't know how to do this alone, I don't like it, and I don't feel good at it. After spending twenty-four years connected to Michael in every area of my life, the adjustment to life without him is like learning to drive a stick shift for the first time: I experience jerky, awkward stalls, and sometimes the engine just shuts down.

It seems that everywhere I turn, I see or experience something that continues to remind me I am no longer part of a pair; I am but one. I even experience it while I fill out an on-line application for Michael Anthony to attend summer camp. There are seven pages with many questions to answer. I come to a box that has marital status options: married, single, divorced, or widowed. It stares back at me. I feel my whole body move into that familiar numbing zone. I halt, and my fingers freeze on the keys, refusing to click on an answer. I con-template it for about sixty seconds.

I am not married—not officially anymore—but my heart is still married to Michael. I am not single. Single makes me think that there is not "another half," and I still feel like I am missing my other half. I am not divorced, nor have I chosen to be a single parent. I am widowed. I was married and have lost the one I love. I am a bearer of grief. I obviously know the answer but have to admit it to myself. I am a widow. I take a deep breath, raise my finger, and hit the key on the appropri-ate box.

A simple truth, and yet a harsh, painful reality.

I feel as if I'm an awkward new driver again, stuck in first gear while trying to switch the shift to second, grinding, then hold-ing back. I slowly move forward, but then slam back into first gear when faced with a situation, a moment, or a time of day when I would have been in contact with Michael. We talked or texted frequently, so this first-gear grinding keeps happening. Our texts were often like passing notes in class: "Date night tonight? :) Yes?" or "Thinking of you" or a simple "I love you" all by itself.

Old habits die hard.

Like tonight after dinner.

Some friends have us over for dinner. Adrienne is in town spending time with me and drives us there. There are some smiles and conversations. I make it through the evening without crying, in spite of the heaviness I feel growing in the pit of my stomach. We get in the car to go home. Instinctively, I reach for my phone from my purse pocket—because Michael hasn't been with us tonight and I need to touch base with him. I want to talk with him and see what he's doing. He's probably sent me a text to check in. I'm about to look for a text update from him when my body slams into first gear—my stomach begins to grind. I catch my thoughts and actions. I feel foolish. Embarrassed with myself, I realize that my old habit of checking in with Michael when he was out of town has kicked in, and there will be no text from him tonight.

I'm shocked at myself. I'm shocked at the human body that responds with such deeply ingrained habits no matter the circumstances. How can my brain actually do this, in spite of the reality? I feel the familiar weight drop deeper into my stomach. Crying, I realize that this part of our relationship is over, too. I'm thankful Adrienne is with me, and that she is driving. I suddenly miss him—desperately—and yearn for just a little text from him.

I saved all of our texting conversations. Tonight I decide to look at them. I discover one in particular he sent me on December 31, 2010. After I read it the first time, I immediately handed the phone to Julie, who was standing nearby in my kitchen, saying, "I have such a great husband!" His text read, "This year will be a year of renewal, discovery, and satisfaction! You will shine this year and I will be right there to polish you each time you grow dull. I love you!!"

I read it again. I'm crying and speechless. I have grown dull and could use some polishing right now.

Experiencing the absence of text messages and phone calls from Michael is not the only time I find myself grinding in first gear. I can't even write on my laptop without a reminder that I am now one—and alone.

I was the last person in our family to have my own laptop. Each of the kids has one for certain school subjects, music programs, and games. I used the "family" computer, an older desktop, which was as slow as Christmas. Michael always had the latest Apple computer for work. Our plan was for me to have my own this year so I could start some writing projects that have been stirring around in me for years. Michael gave me some writing books and screenwriting software for Christmas to get me started on my new endeavors in 2011. Things unfolded much differently this year.

I received *his* laptop on Wednesday night, February 23, 2011.

It had escaped the accident without any harm. His Italian leather satchel, the slouching elephant still sitting in the corner of my room, was returned to me exactly as he had packed it, without anything missing or damaged. Inside the bag, amid many business papers, were the current book he was reading, *Tender Warrior* by Stu Weber (which was a Valentine's Day gift from me), his Italian leather sketchbook and journal, and his laptop. My writing this year is consumed with memories, thoughts, questions, and emotions revolving around our life together and his death, all written on his laptop. My writing books and the copy of Final Draft are collecting dust as they sit on the floor of my bedroom. Such a turn of events.

Michael had various reminders set up on his computer that popped up to help him remember weekly events, like *Date Night with Jené*. For years, our standing date night was every Thursday. Friday nights we celebrated the weekend with the kids and usually had company over for dinner. On Saturday nights, we grilled out on the patio. We liked all of us to have a good night's sleep for church the next morning. We didn't go out every Thursday, but it was good to know that if we wanted to get out, we had the escape route planned. We had lots of dates during the months of November and December because it was when we did all of our Christmas shopping together. After meeting for appetizers and a glass of wine, we hit the shopping. Those nights felt like we were giddy and dating again. If we traveled in those months, we shopped in big cities or quaint little villages.

As on so many other days, today the reminder pops up as I write: *Date Night with Jené*. Wonderful memories come back to me, but I'm instantly reminded that date nights with Jené are over.

Tonight I get ready in my closet to have dinner at a friend's house. My memories of our date nights surface to my thoughts. It's the time of day when I heard the sound of his dress shoes on the hardwood floors of our room as he carried in our date drink. Getting ready tonight is not the same.

I don't know how long I'm going to keep his reminders set up on the laptop. Right now, even though it's difficult, I like to see the order to his life and the priorities he had in place.

I drive to the pet store with my friend Beth. She asks me a simple question: "So, what kind of dog food do you buy?" I open my mouth to say, "Well, we—" I stop short. My body is burning; my tongue is mute. I cry over the question about what kind of dog food I buy.

Certain questions are difficult to answer. Seemingly simple, basic questions about life, not even ones that should stir up emotions, turn into inner turmoil for me. Questions that require an answer like "Well, we do (this or that)" get my heart in a knot. The questions are about something I am presently doing, not something *we* did in the past, so the answer should be an easy *I*. But by habit I answer *we*. As soon as the word rolls off my tongue the wave train blindsides me, as if it's maliciously jeering at me: *You are no longer a* we! *You are all alone now!* I keep my thoughts and emotions to myself in these situations, even after the wave train knocks me in the gut.

Again, old habits die hard.

I begin answering Beth's question about dog food, "Well, we buy…," and the wave train strikes. I pause about ten seconds. I deliberate whether I'm going to let my emotions go there. Because I'm in the safety of a friend, I break. I tell her how hard it is to stop saying "we." I drive down the interstate, tears streaming down my face. Beth quietly holds my arm and cries with me.

Two shall become one takes on a whole new meaning. When we married, we said, "I do." We were separate people who came together as one. We each agreed to the same charge: *'til death do us part.* The "I do" became a "We do" for the rest of our lives together. We were a team. I miss our "we." It truly is a miracle—a miracle that two can become one.

I do.

We did.

Now, I will.

Now I go only to God with *all* of my moments of weakness; He is my safe place. He was always my safe place, but I leaned on Michael for strength as well, and now God is my *only* safe place. In reality, He was always my only *true* safe place—because He is the only thing that never changes. He *is* my strong tower whom I run to when I'm overwhelmed with life—the big things, the small things, and even the seemingly insignificant things.

I begin praying simple prayers. They're scattered throughout the day like little muttered conversations with God. *Lord, Jesus, I need you to come into this place of weakness right now; give me strength.* This seems to be a daily prayer. Exposing that weakness to another human being is also a necessity. I have some people who allow me the opportunity and the security to be weak in their presence. God also uses my pastor, Mike Campbell, as a safe place to share my fears and weaknesses. I feel like another burden lifts after I share it with someone else.

I miss that ever-present feeling of protection I received from Michael: physical, mental, and spiritual. He constantly looked out for the children and me. His prayers, his presence, his actions, and his words gave us a sense of security. I feel exposed without him. I've always known God gives this kind of security, too, but now my faith goes to new heights as I'm forced to lean on Him for *all* of it and not able to see the physical presence of that security anymore. Living every hour of every day as a widow, without the one who was constantly by my side—literally or figuratively—causes me to shrink back timidly and question every move I make. But my faith and dependence on God are emerging stronger than my fears.

CHAPTER 8

Sustaining Love

Bereavement is a universal and integral part of our
experience of love. It follows as normally as marriage
follows courtship or as autumn follows summer. It is
not a truncation of the process but one of its phases;
not the interruption of the dance, but the next figure.

—C. S. Lewis, *A Grief Observed*

T HE GRIEVING PROCESS IS CYCLICAL but feels more like a spiral
moving me forward—forward and back, forward and back. I
wrote feverishly on my blog through each of these moments,
recording every detailed memory of life with Michael. It was
my way of focusing in the midst of the overwhelming waves.

Yesterday I pulled away for most of the day to write in my
bedroom. In and out of writing, there were occasional conversations with my parents, who are here for a visit. Tonight they
sit quietly in my kitchen, along with Julie, as I put dinner together. It's been a melancholy day.

My activity in the kitchen doesn't qualify as cooking—at
least not for me. They all know this is my first time preparing a

meal without Michael, even though so many months have passed. It's hard beginning the process tonight, as small as it is.

I put a ham in the oven, get the corn ready to steam in a pan, and make the mint tea. *Stay in motion, Jené—just get it done.* I set out everything for the tomato pies. The heavy sadness descends on me, making it difficult to move. My thoughts of Michael take my mind away from the cooking process. My dad wants to put some music on the iPod speakers and says he's in the mood for some "good ole" American standards. He chooses Rod Stewart's *The Great American Songbook*.

I disappear completely into my thoughts.

It's the five o'clock hour. Wine and quiet conversation mingle with the culinary aromas of dinner, bringing the senses together...just like they always did. Rod Stewart's American Songbook plays in the kitchen...just like it always did.

"Every time we say goodbye, I die a little."

The music once brought peace to my soul, stirred my dreams, ushered in a spirit of serenity at the close of a day. Tonight it sinks in my stomach as the lump in my throat grows. A wave of absolute loneliness hits me. You're not here—neither is the peace, or the dreams, or the serenity. My legs are unstable. My ears are ringing. I feel as if I'm falling to the ground in slow motion.

"Every time we say goodbye, I die a little."

Every time I experience something we once did together, I say good-bye to you...over and over again. Part of my heart dies with each good-bye. Other voices now fill the air while I cook my first meal since you've been gone, but I hear only the silence where your voice once filled me, like a deep breath. Now I can't breathe. It's just the three of us: Rod Stewart, your absence, and me.

"Every time we say goodbye, I die a little."

I realize I *did* die a little, but one day, someday, my breath will return, beauty will return, life will return.

Everything is present for a good evening, but it doesn't feel good. There's ambience but I don't recognize it. I sense only loneliness; each movement I make is strained. The joy once here when Michael was in and out of the kitchen is gone. With the exception of the music, it's fairly quiet in the kitchen now. I'm not in the mood to talk. Julie talks with Dad while she opens a bottle of wine. I hear the lyrics rise above their talk: "I'll be seeing you / in all the old, familiar places..."

It takes on a whole new meaning for me.

Michael loved drinking a glass of wine in the kitchen while I cooked. Instead of Michael sitting at the kitchen counter tonight, it's my mom sitting in his place. She watches me slowly move dinner along. I feel as if I'm the only one in the room, with the sound of the music playing somewhere off in the distance. I decide to put on an apron.

In my trance, I pick out an apron and thoughtfully put it over my head. Michael bought me this apron about twenty years ago, from our favorite restaurant at the time. We ate our celebratory dinner at this restaurant after learning I was pregnant with Mia. I realize this is the first time I have put on the apron since February 21, our last family dinner together. I made manicotti and we ate on the patio while listening to Rod Stewart.

No one is aware of the distance my thoughts have journeyed since the music began. To them, I appear busy with the task of cooking, but I'm a robot doing what my body knows to do in the kitchen while my mind is free to wander elsewhere. I fight the tears. My strength to keep the dam from bursting is waning. I turn around as Julie passes a glass of wine to me—she holds up her glass to offer a toast to me. I instinctively take the glass. She announces, "A toast to another first."

The dam bursts.

I break down, shaking my head while looking into her eyes. I can't do it. I held in my private world of thoughts long enough and cannot pretend a moment longer. I catch my breath. The room goes completely silent with the exception of Rod in the background. The others join me in the grieving of the moment. No one says anything. What can you say? They hug me, let me cry, and cry with me—which is exactly what we need.

The reality of life without Michael sets in, one experience at a time. No matter how much strength I gain with each passing day, memories of Michael overwhelm me continually. They leave me standing there, stunned by grief. The wave train hit tonight with a force I wasn't expecting. Moments like these still catch me off guard in the most unlikely places—like in the dentist's office. A simple trip for a checkup was like climbing Mount Everest.

We are in a strict habit of going to the dentist as a family every six months to get our teeth cleaned. It was recently that time again. After deliberating if I was up to seeing more people for the first time since Michael's death, I decided to forge through it. There was nothing I could have done to prevent my emotions and thoughts from overcoming me while sitting in the dentist's chair that day.

I sit in the waiting room with Michael Anthony with self-talk in my head: *Okay. This is a peaceful, safe environment. I love these people and they love me. I can do this. It isn't going to be too bad; I mean, it's the dentist's office, right?* They call me to go back.

The familiar weight pushes down on my chest and stomach. I silently sit in the chair. Small talk is *not* a good idea. It feels as if an elephant is in this tiny room. It's sitting on me, stealing all of the oxygen. Even though the music plays quietly in the background, the atmosphere is profoundly silent. I stare at a painting of white clouds on a background of blue hanging on the wall in front of me. I'm disappearing into it. It's the only thing I see. Sensing my mood, the hygienist is tender and spares me the small talk.

It's time for X-rays.

She places the heavy bib on me. I notice something's missing: Is there any possibility you could be pregnant?—the standard question for women right before an X-ray. I see the wave swell before impact. I brace myself as it crushes over my mind. It's the first time in twenty-four years I don't need to be concerned about the possibility of being pregnant.

A new grief is observed. I realize in an instant that along with losing Michael, my hope of having more children has died with him as well.

After one year of marriage, Michael and I agreed not to use any form of birth control. Having faith in God in all other areas of our lives, we decided to trust Him with this area as well. If we trusted Him with our very lives, our future, our health, our salvation, our finances, we could certainly trust Him with this. We released our birth control and gave God the control instead, letting Him decide how many biological children we would have and when they would come. We felt secure in our decision.

Our children were spaced out in a way over which we had no control. Four years after our decision to let God have our birth control, we had Mia. Another four years later, Julia, and then Michael Anthony quickly came in last. I weaned Julia at eleven months and the next month was pregnant. Michael and I always felt we were destined to have five or six children. Every month I wondered, *Is this going to be the month?* Months and years went by, but additional pregnancies never came. Every night in bed, Michael wrapped his arms around me or held my hands and prayed over our family—including a petition for more children.

Around 2007, we separately felt during our private prayer times that we were to pursue adoption. Michael's prayers at night slightly changed. He began to pray for protection over the children who were already out there—the children God would choose to bring into our family. We had a private adoption fall through in 2009. The sixteen-year-old mother changed her mind after she gave birth, and left the hospital with the baby girl. We had named her Sophia Grace. We continued praying for her protection. It took me a year to put away the pink blankets, the bassinet, and the clothing I'd purchased with the children on a shopping trip. The next year we became foster parents to the precious little boy we had until the time of Michael's death. Although our home was not his "forever

GOOD NIGHT, I LOVE YOU

home," God entrusted us with his heart. We were a safe place and a connecting bridge to his future home.

As I sit in the dentist's chair, my mind runs like a freight train through all of these memories in a matter of sixty seconds.

Last year I switched over to a female ob-gyn. I told her that Michael and I agreed we were content with not having any more biological children and were ready to look at other options. I remember her asking me, "Are you sure? Don't you just want to know *why* you haven't had any children?"

We agreed to run some tests in an attempt to answer the outstanding medical question. I took some medicine that would raise my progesterone levels if I was ovulating, which meant my side of the deal was good. The doctor called me with the results, and her excitement came through the phone: "Your levels are through the roof!" She then suggested we have Michael tested to make sure all was well in his department. He texted me on February 2 and told me his levels were all normal—only twenty days before he died. We were instructed to give it a go.

We followed the doctor's orders but were willing to walk away from it because we had a peace about it in our hearts. Our time of "trying" took us right up to two nights before the wreck. After receiving the news of his death, I immediately carried this additional, huge secret burden. I cried out to God on my bed, *Oh, dear God! Please! I know I have been a strong woman in the past, but please don't make me do this! Please! I don't think I can carry his child for the next nine months without him by my side. Lord have mercy, Lord have mercy!*

I had to wait before I knew the answer. I started my period and it came early—for the first time in my whole marriage. God was merciful, and had been all along. I broke down, relieved, yet so sad at the same time. This Scripture came to my mind from Jeremiah 29:11: "'For I know the plans I have for you,' declares the LORD, 'plans to prosper you and not to harm you, plans to give you hope and a future'" (NIV). There was never anything wrong with us; God simply knew best.

The memories all went back to a heavy bib in the dentist's chair.

This morning is busy at an early hour. Emma Claire, my niece, spent the night. It's seven thirty, and I'm feeding her breakfast before she goes to preschool. Mia has to be at work at eight. My dad left a couple of days ago, and today my mom prepares to leave. She's leaving at the same time Emma Claire needs to go to school but has just inadvertently locked the keys in her car while packing. Now she waits for a locksmith to arrive. I'm expecting a delivery of Michael Anthony's new bed at any moment. In the middle of all of this, I decide to call my father-in-law to tell him about a Boy Scout project coming up for the boys to earn a large number of community service hours. He was Michael's Scoutmaster when he was a boy and wants to stay informed about Michael Anthony's Scouting experience.

I pick up the phone—my fingers automatically dial Michael's cell phone number. I almost finish punching in the entire number before I catch what I'm doing. Standing in the kitchen, I freeze while all of the commotion surrounds me. I stare at the phone. The numbers blare back at me. My world closes in on me for about thirty seconds, though it seems longer. My chest grows heavy. Tears well up in my eyes—I hold them while I stare. What made me do that? Was it being alone in the kitchen on a busy morning, when in the past I would have called him during that moment to ask a question or for an opinion? Was it because I was calling someone to talk about Boy Scouts? Was it just a morning habit resurfacing since we always talked shortly after he left in the morning? Was it because we always shared the load on busy days through communication?

Looking at his number on the screen somehow makes me feel like he's within reach. I don't understand it. He was always on the other end of the line anytime I needed him. If he couldn't talk, he'd quickly send me a text to answer any question. I take a deep breath, clear the numbers, and dial my in-laws. I want to tell my mother-in-law what just happened. I want to cry with her. I choose to keep moving and talk about Boy Scouts. This morning has moved right along, but now I choke and sputter, like a car running out of gas.

I keep my thoughts inside as my mom bustles around and Emma Claire sings songs—because it's what I need to do in this moment. Later, I give myself permission to come back to all of these feelings when I'm alone, in the closet. I examine the moment. I call Michael's number just to make it complete. I listen to his voice message. I'm glad it's still there. I just needed to call him, so I did.

It's been eight months, and the closet is still a huge wall to scale. I decide to poke around in his clothes and shoes—they remain as he left them. I need a moment to think about him. In an instant, I realize I've been living in a time warp. For the first time I notice dust collecting on the folds of his pants and on the tops of his suit coats. My thoughts speak to him in a one-way conversation, as if he's listening. I touch his clothes. *You were such a great dresser. You are really gone, aren't you? Where are you? What are you doing now? I miss you. You are not coming back. How am I doing as a single parent?*

It is silent.

There is no big onslaught of tears. My eyes fill, but hold there. I'm melancholy with reminiscent thoughts of missing him and the sight of him in his fabulous clothes.

I pull out his shoes to look at them. I find an obvious layer of dust there as well. I snap forward from the time warp. He's been gone a long time. It seems he was here just a short time ago. This is all still so fresh—how can it have been eight months? The dust speaks the reality. It's time to begin the cleaning-out process. His dresser drawers are still full of his clothes, and his winter sweaters are in a container under our bed.

Last week I organized my side of the closet with the help of my niece. Jennings is in her twenties and has always loved to help create order. It was my way of taking a baby step toward doing Michael's clothes. Even going through my clothes was hard, because so many memories of him are wrapped up in every piece of my clothing—him choosing it, where we were when I wore it with him, how much he liked it on me, and the comments he made about each item when something really pleased him. He was full of compliments. It's difficult to get rid of things I know he loved.

I can't decide whether I'll edge my clothes over to the other side once I finish going through his clothes. I like the discipline it takes to keep the clothes I own down to a number that fits into my tiny space. Maybe I'll use some of his side for storage. At first I didn't feel so alone as long as his clothes still hung in the closet, where they belonged—like a false protection. But now, as the dust collects on them, it's the opposite. They bring attention to the stark fact: I *am* alone. They weigh on me. They are like a shadow lurking in the other side of the closet. It's depressing. It feels stagnant. I think their presence keeps me from moving forward.

Dust represents the fact that something is forgotten, neglected, or abandoned. As I see the dust on his things, I'm reminded that these things are abandoned. Moving forward is not something I have wanted to do, but now, as the dust collects, I realize I must move forward in small steps like this or life cannot return. The clothes represent a past life. A life that was, but is no more.

The closet hasn't been the only wall that looms in front of me. I still haven't touched the elephant sitting in the corner of my room—the ottoman with the random assortment of items, each carrying an incredible amount of emotional weight. Like Michael's clothes, they've been collecting dust since the week following his accident.

His Italian leather satchel and leather notebook still lie dormant in the pile. Also collecting dust is a huge Ziploc bag of loose items taken from his car, a large manila envelope with EVIDENCE BAG printed across it containing proof that it was he who had died (wallet, crucifix necklace, wedding ring, car insurance card, etc.), his camera bag, copies of the newspaper with the article about his accident on the front page, a large envelope of letters from the Boy Scout troop, and the Bose system from his desk at his office. It's all covered in a thin layer of dust.

His broken glasses that once sat on top of the pile were now tucked away in his personal catchall drawer. I didn't have the strength to put away any more than his glasses that day. Just as his clothes once brought me comfort, the whole pile of things on the ottoman made me feel as if he wasn't so far away and hadn't been gone too long. As time passed, though, a change took place. The sight of his dusty personal items heaped all over the ottoman torments me. Everything brings the trauma to my memory in a split second if I glance in that direction. It's a shadow lurking in the corner of my room, just like the closet.

A mountain. Immovable. Ominous. Looming. Towering.

Today I stand at the base of this mountain, looking at its daunting complexity.

For the sake of my mental health, it's time to scale the mountain and put it all away. I want and need my room to be a calm, safe place. Of course, the empty feeling will remain because I'm alone in it. I can at least put away anything relating to his death, even what he was reading leading up to his death, like the books that still sit on his nightstand.

It took Michael months to finish books, because he meditated on what he read for a long time. While reading deeper books, he read about one page, then wanted to talk about it. He worked out his thoughts for another couple of days, bringing them into conversations with other people, then moved on in the book.

I look at his nightstand now and see what he was reading and what he planned on reading next. These books have remained unopened for eight months but now will go back into my library for future reading. They range in his three favorite topics: spiritual, parenting, and architecture.

My nightstand is stocked full of my own books, which have not been touched in eight months, either. Reading is still hard for me. It requires me to turn off my thoughts, which is not yet possible. It's difficult to focus on anything—fiction, nonfiction, the Bible, magazine articles, really anything. I picked up playing Words with Friends on my phone when I get into bed at night. It's a light distraction. I have high hopes of beginning to read again soon. I have enough in my books-to-read-next pile to last me over a year.

For now, I chip away at the glass-dust-covered mountain and move his books to the library downstairs. I know God will be with me every moment of it, as He has been up to this point. His grace is sufficient for me, just like He said it would be. The task is hard but a good step forward.

As the number of readers on my blog grew, I began getting "fan" mail from strangers. Several people even called my home wanting to know if they could meet me while they were in town; they had a shared experience or wanted advice. I learned that people were using the blog for group Bible studies and prayer groups, and couples were even using it as their daily devotional together. Everywhere I turned, people said things like

"You have such a ministry with this blog" or "You are helping so many people." Every time I heard these words, instead of thinking, *Well, praise God!* I began getting bitter toward God: *God, why couldn't I have had a ministry this vast without having to lose my Michael? This isn't fair. It's not fair that other people are benefitting from my pain!* I didn't want to think about my blog as a ministry. It was for the healing of my heart, for my friends and family to have insight into my heart, and for my children to have the detailed memories I wrote about our lives with their father.

Yet the more I wrote, the more sustaining the memories themselves were. From the days of our courtship through the raising of our children, Michael's love had nourished me. It was still there, *is* still there, even as I feel his loss. Somehow, the more I missed him, the stronger I became. Just as building up an immunity to something comes from repeated exposure to it, the more I was confronted with his memory, the more accustomed I became to his absence and the better I held my ground with each crashing wave.

The more I remembered, the more I recognized the strength and depth of the faith we had together. I became more determined not to lose it. God and I remained mostly silent, but constantly kept a close watch on one another. My faith had smoldered, but never extinguished. The flames began to rise again in my soul. Yes, I was still walking through the darkness and experiencing the Midnight Hour, but as the wave train continued to hit my heart, I rose back to my feet with determination, my head up even though there were tears in my eyes. Each time I had to make an intentional decision: I will not back down from my faith. I refuse to drown.

CHAPTER 9

One Shall Become Two

Therefore a man shall leave his father and his mother
and shall become united *and* cleave to his wife, and
they shall become one flesh.

—GENESIS 2:24 (AMPC)

I MENTALLY PREPARE FOR TODAY, the annual piano recital for the tenth consecutive year. It's Mia's tenth and final recital, also referred to as her senior recital, Julia's seventh, Michael Anthony's fifth, and my first to attend without their father. Piano lessons are not an option in our home. Michael took piano lessons from his grandmother when he was young, and his recitals were held in the same little art museum where our children now have theirs.

They had little focus this year when, and if, they practiced. They missed some lessons and went weeks without any practice at all. Julia practiced more than the other two—it appears to be therapeutic for her. Her piece this year is *Sunflowers and Wheat Fields* by Catherine Rollin, an enchanting and moving score. It sounds like a theme song to a dramatic movie. I cry as I hear its notes float throughout the house while she practices. Mia chose Beethoven's *Moonlight Sonata* for her final recital. It evokes emotion as well, but with a different kind of weight from Julia's selection. It swells and builds throughout the piece but sounds like sadness and loneliness. Michael Anthony will play Bach's Minuet in G Major, a happy piece, and fitting for his personality.

All three pleaded with me to let them drop out of the recital. They felt they couldn't sufficiently prepare. All the pieces had to be memorized. None of them knew the pieces in their entirety until last week. I knew in my heart that they could do it and felt the process of preparation would be good for them. Mia was stressed not only over the piece itself, but also because it was her senior recital and the audience would expect something great.

The student performing the senior recital is always the grand finale to the recital. Under the circumstances, Mia's teacher placed her third from the end to help lift some pressure. Julia knows her piece but is concerned she may feel overwhelmed with the need to cry while she plays. Her whole personality changed in the last few days as the recital quickly approached. She felt the magnitude of the moment long before it happened. Michael is ready but doesn't want to do it simply because the girls don't. I asked all of them to play this year as if it were a gift to me—to their dad. Their souls need to play as much as mine needs to hear them. I see it as part of this grieving process for all of us.

The kids load up in Mia's car to arrive early for the recital. The house is a vacuum of silence. Today I don't trust my ability to hold it together in public. The tears brim in my eyes, and

I'm not even there yet. My arms become weighted with grief as I apply makeup to my wet eyes. Compelled to pray for the children, I talk to God as if He's standing right here with me. I ask Him to help them play with beauty and grace. *God, let courage abound!*

So far, experiencing these proud parenting moments alone hasn't gotten any easier.

I arrive, and the three of them sit side by side in the holding area. The girls look so beautiful, mature, and peaceful. Michael Anthony is handsome in his Sunday-best clothes and sits calmly beside Julia. I kiss each one on the cheek and tell them how proud I am—no matter what. I am proud of them simply for coming.

Armed with tissues, I sit down with my mom and Craig. I give him video instructions so I can focus on the music. I listen to seventeen other children perform, but then Michael Anthony strolls across the front toward the stage looking handsome and sure. Where is my little boy? He sits down and begins the minuet. He makes a small mistake shortly into it; without missing a beat, he begins the piece again. I swell with pride. My lungs fill with fresh air. This young man is intensely focused on the keys as he plays the grand piano. The same young man who fights Airsoft wars in the neighborhood. The same young man who rides his bike, catches fish, shoots guns, builds Legos, and plays tennis. He is living a balanced life—just like his dad. Completing a near-perfect performance, he stands and takes a bow. I feel a sigh of relief and can't help but smile at my young man.

Six other performances to gear myself up for the next one.

Julia enters wearing a hot pink, floor-length, flowing skirt. I know by the way she carries herself that she's going to nail it. I make it through the first ten seconds, but then the tears flow. It's beautiful, she's beautiful, and the music successfully transports everyone here to a lovely, beautiful memory. I catch my breath because of my tears.

I'm in awe of her strength to perform. I'm in awe of Michael Anthony's perseverance to perform. I grieve for Michael, our Renaissance man who would've relished this moment, who would've cried tears of pride right beside me. Julia flows as she touches the keys with gentleness, recognizing the emotion behind each note. The song leaves me drifting as she takes her bow and quickly casts a glance my way. I'm relieved to see I have two more people before Mia. I'm a mess.

Mia enters. I instantly realize that she now looks like a college girl. She sits on the bench, and my memory floods with visions of her through the years sitting on that same bench in all of the special dresses chosen for the occasion. When she was younger, I hand-sewed the dresses. Now, she wears a soft green dress she chose from J.Crew. She glows. I picture her long hair pulled back with a ribbon like she wore it in recitals long past. She thoughtfully takes a moment, then begins to play. Her peace and confidence are palpable. She takes her time and moves her body with the mood of the music.

I feel as if I cried myself out on Julia's piece. Sitting peacefully, I soak up the moment as Mia plays the sounds of her heart; then the tears return. Where has the time gone? Is this really her senior recital? How did she learn to play like that? She looks so mature. She's pulled it all together, against all odds. She overcame. Our first child, and what a tender heart she has. She touches the keys as if they're old friends, yet commands them at the same time. She decided ahead of time that if she makes a mistake, the only ones who will notice are her piano teacher and I. She takes some creative liberties, and no one is the wiser. Moving all over the keys with constant control, her fingers hover and flow through the eight-minute piece. Her touch brings the gravity of the piece to all of us. The final notes bring the feeling of completion. It is finished. Standing to take her bow, she gives me a loving smile.

I want to run down the aisle and pick them all up in my arms and tell them how amazing they are, how proud I am of their accomplishment. I hold the impulse and wipe the remaining tears. I notice I'm not the only one in the crowd crying. Most everyone knows of our loss and how difficult today is for us. One woman tells me she prayed for me while they played. The three of them are beaming.

This is the first of many accomplishments without Michael present to share in the moment. They strengthened me with their strength today. They strengthened me with their gift. They strengthened all of us with the beauty they bring to this world—and by sharing their beauty, they strengthened themselves.

I recently talked to my brother-in-law, Johnny, who lost his wife to cancer two years before Michael died. He has two daughters the same ages as mine. We discussed how parenting presents new challenges after losing your mate. He said it's difficult as a single parent to meet their needs because now it's only one person doing the job that once took two to do somewhat successfully. My thoughts continue on with that thought.

I see the irony in this well-known verse, Mark 10:8: "and the two shall become one flesh" (ESV). Now it's turned around: one shall become two. One must now run a household that took two before. Picking up the children, attending events, taking them places: one shall do the work of two. One must now discern and recognize their emotional needs, when it took two sets of eyes and two hearts before. Single parenting—it's a miracle it can be done at all, never mind done successfully. I recognize this and know it's only the grace of God working through me, guiding me through every detail, and girding me with the strength and perseverance it takes.

It's Sunday afternoon, and I have a "date" with my children on my bed. My heart is full with things to share. We rarely have the opportunity to gather together with only the four of us. I share my hurts and frailties. I tell them the tears and pain will continue to come for all of us. *Let them.* I tell them they may feel like crying a year or two years from now. *This is okay.* We will continue to miss him. Experiencing life without him will be hard. Going to new places without him may be hard, going to old places may be hard, birthdays may be hard, and graduations may be hard. *Know this going into the rest of your life.* He will be missed, and the tears may arise at unexpected moments. I encourage them to give their emotions freedom for the rest of their days.

I pray with them. I cry with them.

I apologize in advance for failing. I tell them there will be times I fail as a parent. I am one person trying to meet their needs when it once took two. I tell them not to wait for me to come to them to meet a need. I may sometimes miss it. *Come to me and I will come to you.* I tell them their father parented and met their needs in ways slightly different than my ways. We filled in the gaps for each other. Now it's just me.

I pray to God to show me how one shall parent as two did before.

I know God also uses other people to fill in some of these gaps. For example, Michael Anthony has a need for physical touch through roughhousing. He and his dad wrestled, had Nerf gun wars inside the house, chased and scared each other, practiced defensive football stances in the front yard, and dunked one another in the pool. The girls have frequently stepped into this role, as well as a couple of men. Even though other people may occasionally step in to meet a need, the responsibility of daily living, loving, guiding, and walking together through this life ultimately falls on me.

One person filling the gap and meeting their needs that once took two—an enlightening realization that two really did become one flesh. Because Michael and I were one flesh, I learned from him and he learned from me, a holistic approach of loving our children as a team. I learned from him to recognize certain needs I may not have seen without him. I now parent as one *because* we became one flesh. Because we spent twenty-four years watching one another parent, I now see the children through his eyes as well. I now have character qualities and abilities because two became one. That union now allows me, only one, to parent as two—because two became one flesh, and that one flesh will continue.

I have cried more since Michael's death than I have in all my living days. David says in Psalm 56:8, "You keep track of all my sorrows. You have collected all my tears in your bottle" (NLT). My bottle now overflows. Most of my tears are from grief. Some tears are shed in the presence of sheer loneliness. Some tears are for the children's loss of their fun-loving father. Others are shed at God's feet for help. Today I recognize tears of a different kind—tears from the overwhelming weight of being a parent and the significance it carries.

This is a good sign, really. Some parents may never feel this significance. Parenting takes prayer, planning, and a disciplined life. The details matter. Daily decisions matter. Prayers over the children matter. The friends they keep matter. Guiding them matters. Teaching them communication skills and how to forgive and respect others matters. Setting an example for them matters. Listening and understanding them matters. All of this carries more magnitude for me now that the responsibility falls solely on me. I've always been passionate about my role as a parent, taking every decision to God and to Michael for discussion. Raising children to glorify God with their lives and to love people with no boundaries is the most important job God has given me. This has not changed.

It's a bad sign if I no longer feel this significance, a sign I'm giving up on life. I have no intention of giving up. I'm "fighting the good fight of faith." I understand that quote from Paul better now. It *is* a fight and I *must* battle for it daily. There are pain and tears in most every fight. I pull through this battle *because* of my faith. It stands out before me as my shield in battle.

Today I pull out one of the Scripture cards from the stack on my nightstand. I'm reminded that God really is with me, fighting for me. He says:

"Fear not, for I have redeemed you; I have called you by name, you are mine. When you pass through the waters, I will be with you; and through the rivers, they shall not overwhelm you; when you walk through fire you shall not be burned, and the flame shall not consume you" (Isa. 43:1–2 ESV).

The only reason parenting doesn't consume me is because God is with me. The tears I shed are easier to handle because I know He sees them and gathers them. The pain is hard no matter what. God doesn't take the tears or pain away, but he carries me *through* the circumstances.

I run into a friend at my favorite gardening store while looking for flowers to plant in my side garden. I'm still not gardening—I can't bring myself to garden yet without Michael. I'll have someone else plant them for me. Mimi and her husband, Allen, own the garden center. It's my first time seeing her since Michael died. We talk a few minutes, and I comfortably tear up right in the middle of the flowers. She tells me she prays for us and then mentions a profound truth: at a time in my life when I am my absolute weakest, I must also be my absolute strongest, for the sake of the children. The juxtaposition amazes me every day. How can these two extremes coexist? Strength to weakness, weakness to strength.

I believe it's only possible because of the abundance of intercessory prayers going to God on behalf of my children and me—like Mimi's prayers. Every day I hear that someone else prays for us. Churches pray for us, distant acquaintances pray for us, even strangers pray for us. At times I'm overwhelmed to tears when a stranger is introduced to me and recognizes my name, then grabs my arm and says, "Jené, how are you? I've been praying for you." God's grace covers me daily and enables me to perform this dance back and forth between strength and weakness.

I'm weak in areas I've never in my life been weak in before. I've always been somewhat of a "Wonder Woman." Now I'm fragile. I cry with the change of the wind. I hurt inside every minute of every day. It's always there, hovering beneath the surface, no matter what I'm doing, no matter how my mood appears. Coexisting are the capabilities to do things and pull through emotionally for my children with strength I don't know is within me. I have been a strong person all my life, but now God has taken that strength to supernatural levels to carry us through our day-to-day living.

He gives me emotional strength when the children need to see me emotionally strong, physical strength when they need me present and doing things with them, spiritual strength when they need to know that God is still in control, that I still trust in Him with my whole heart, and that we are stable and secure in our little family unit.

Today I bounce from weakness to strength to weakness. It's Youth Sunday at church. Mia is singing the special music. At the beginning of the service, we all sing, "I Am a Friend of God." This was "Michael's" song; he usually led this song in church. As soon as the music starts, I impatiently dig through my purse for tissues. I find them, prepare myself, and then look up to see that Mia is no longer onstage with the choir. She's standing between the piano and the front row, head down, hands covering her face as the music director consoles her.

I slip out of my row and walk down the aisle to join her. We stand and hold one another, quietly crying together. "This is his song," I whisper, and she nods her head, which is buried in my neck. I ask her if she's okay to sing her song, and she says she can do it. I kiss her one last time and walk to my seat while everyone continues singing.

When I am back at my seat, the strength for Mia disappears. I feel utter weakness—I flee to the restroom without looking at anyone. A woman sees me in the hall and follows me into the restroom. As I step one foot into the ladies' room, I lose it. She immediately holds me as I sob. She cries with me and comforts me. I'm in complete weakness. Five minutes pass; I reach for strength and go back into the sanctuary for Mia's solo. God carries us both through it. She sings beautifully. I'm exhausted. The children know I'm in a weak moment after the service, but they're compassionate. There are times when they feel it, too, and we're comforted existing in the weakness together. At other times they don't want any sadness—they want to experience joy and see my strength.

We dance through this together. Weakness to strength and strength to weakness. God is with us in both. We help one another through the ebb and flow of these contrasting truths.

If it weren't for the children, how easy it could be to stay in weakness and lose all desire to reach for strength. Their very lives make me determined to gather every bit of strength available to me. It's my strong desire to protect and guide them. Parenting is a most beautiful, significant, and challenging journey.

CHAPTER 10

I Choose

> We must be still and still moving
> Into another intensity
> For a further union, a deeper communion
> Through the dark cold and the empty desolation,
> The wave cry, the wind cry, the vast waters
> Of the petrel and the porpoise. In my end is my beginning.
>
> —T. S. ELIOT, *FOUR QUARTETS*

IT'S BEEN ALMOST A YEAR, and my wedding ring is still on my finger. I've decided today is the day. God has provided space and strength for me to remove it—with the help of colder weather. I'm more aware of the ring because of my old habit of spinning it around my finger with my thumb on cold days. I do it all the time—it's time to lay the ring to rest.

Be still and still moving.

This seemingly small act is monumental for me. I feel as if I'm turning to the last page of a fairy-tale book where I see the words "The End" written in a lovely script. In slow motion, the book closes. At this point, people usually think, *What a beautiful story!* Or *It all came together so nicely!* Or even *Nice story, but things don't happen like that in real life*. It's really all these things, because fairy tales never tell the final ending of the story.

A fairy-tale ending is not an ending at all. It's the beginning of a beautiful journey through life together. A beautiful journey through life is beautiful not because everything is perfect. It's beautiful because of the strength, growth, sacrifices, courage, tenacity, and fierce love it takes to overcome hardships on the journey. An overcoming love is the most beautiful love of all. The deeper the love runs because of shared hardships and pain, the lovelier it is.

Authors and speakers John and Stasi Eldredge say, "A healed heart is more glorious than a heart that has never been wounded." My heart will be even more glorious in its scarred state as I walk on in this life. It's healing, but deep wounds leave a scar even after they heal. I walk on without Michael but with the memories of our journey and the heart I shared with him. When I see the fairy tale in its entirety, then I can look at it and say, *Wow, that was really beautiful!*

I drive to the jewelry store where we purchased our rings twenty-five years ago. I meet with Ron, our jeweler. He's expecting me. I remove the ring and hand it to him to clean and inspect the setting. I brought with me a couple of old watches needing repair, a good distraction while I wait for the ring. As I walk around the store, looking in the glass cases at all of the fine jewelry, I finger Michael's wedding band hanging around my neck. I eavesdrop on a couple of men in the store as they choose engagement rings for their girlfriends. Today they open the book of their own fairy-tale journey.

Ron emerges holding my ring, proclaiming that it all looks

good. He beams while he shows me its beauty as it sparkles in the light. We attempt small talk as he packages it for me. He opens a new black velvet ring box, places the ring inside, and then places the ring box within another box. Instantly my strength recedes. I barely breathe—my ears ring.

Be still and still moving.

He finally pulls out a gift bag and places the box down inside. He makes a comment to which I can't reply and gives me a knowing look as he hands me the bag. I have a quick thought that it's similar to the "evidence bag" of items gathered from Michael's car and his body. The original purpose of the ring has died—it's now evidence and proof of a life well lived. Evidence of priorities and values well placed. Evidence of a beautiful life. Beautiful not because it was perfect, but beautiful because of the tenacity and fierce love we maintained through every fire and every victory.

I pull out of the parking lot, and the wave crashes. Driving home, I try holding myself together to some extent. I'm hyperventilating through the tears. What just happened? Was this real? Here I am, driving in lunch-hour traffic, alongside people rushing to get back to work or to the next place to shop for Christmas presents, while my heart wrenches with pain and grieves as I embrace the end of my fairy tale.

At home, I sit on my bed, pull out the ring box, and then flip open the lid. I stare at the ring. I touch it on both sides with my two thumbs while holding the black velvet box in my hands. My mind goes back to the night he proposed to me on Christmas Eve in the restaurant we had all to ourselves.

He reads Mark 10:6–9 (ESV) with his quiet voice:

"But from the beginning of creation, 'God made them male and female.' 'Therefore a man shall leave his father and mother and hold fast to his wife, and the two shall become one flesh.' So they are no longer two but one flesh. What therefore God has joined together, let not man separate."

With tears in his eyes, he gets down on one knee, pulls a gray velvet ring box out of his coat pocket, and then opens it for me to see. Looking at me for the first time is this perfectly chosen ring.

I think about our life story for a while. I see the words on the final page of the fairy tale along with the closing of the book, and then say in my heart, *Wow, that was really beautiful.*

We made it through all of our birthdays for the first time without him. We made it through Easter weekend without him. We made it through the first Christmas without him. I made it through Christmas shopping without him. I made it through my first wedding anniversary without him. Our first New Year's Eve without him was a time of heavy introspection. I kept repeating Isaiah 43:2 as if it were my daily mantra: "When you pass through the waters, I will be with you; and when you pass through the rivers, they will not sweep over you" (NIV).

Be still and still moving.

The morning of my birthday, I dreamed of a gathering with some friends serving up a special birthday brunch for me.

Since it was a birthday without Michael, they tried making it extra special. As I walked toward the gathering, they sang "Happy Birthday." I grabbed my stomach, attempting to fight back the tears, but then doubled over with cries from deep down and stumbled. I awoke at that point. I lay still in the morning silence. One at a time, the kids trickled into my room and gave me a birthday hug.

We have a tradition of birthday breakfasts. I cook whatever the birthday person requests. I set the table the night before and place the wrapped presents down the middle like a flamboyant centerpiece. When the birthday girl or boy walks into the kitchen the next morning, it feels like Christmas. Michael always made sure it was equally done for me on my birthday. Last year he made organic-spelt-flour blueberry scones. He'd never baked anything before but researched a recipe online. He was thrilled to make something he knew I'd love. They were fabulous and, of course, there were lots of presents. His generous spirit came out in full force on birthdays and Christmas. He gave extravagantly.

This year the kids worked together in the kitchen and cooked my birthday breakfast: waffles made from freshly ground spelt flour. The room felt empty without Michael across the table giving me "that look." (Jennings once said if she was in the room when Uncle Michael gave me that look, with our eyes engaged, she felt as if she was interrupting something.) It was beautiful watching the children make it special for me. I was amazed by and proud of their fortitude. God carried their hearts in the palm of His hand.

We had another tradition for birthday lunch: heading to

Brent's Drugs to eat in their Soda Fountain diner. Michael joined us from work and took his time with his Brent's Burger and large vanilla malt. The kids ordered hamburgers with Cokes or milk shakes, and I always ordered a tuna melt or an egg-and-olive sandwich. (You have to experience it to know how good it really is.) I allowed the children to "skip" school on their birthdays, which made it even more special. Nothing was the same for my birthday lunch this year. A group of my friends took me to lunch, Mia had a college algebra class and a haircut, Julia ate with Craig, and Michael Anthony ate with our youth pastor.

Michael's was the last birthday to experience in his absence. Had he been with us, there would have been Magic Marshmallow Puffs and bacon welcoming everyone down for the birthday breakfast. I would have woken him with a birthday kiss; it was one of the few days in the year he slept a little later. The rest of the morning would've been full of love, laughter, good food, and all of Michael's comments as he opened presents. With each present, he shrugged his shoulders and wrinkled up his nose with a smile, showing us all pure satisfaction over the gift.

I made an Italian cream cake every November 14 for over twenty years. There was no cake this year. I did not cook his favorite birthday meal of veal, smoked sausage, bacon, and sage over angel hair pasta. The day ended with takeout salads from a local restaurant. I went to bed early. The day was finally over. I lay in silence that evening, remembering all these things. Life is going on.

Be still and still moving.

Just when I thought I was actually fully accepting his death, the Christmas holidays hit.

I heard my thoughts saying, *Is this real?* Weren't the kids and I just sitting on the couch together watching him meticulously string the Christmas lights on the tree? Didn't we just do our evening Christmas shopping spree together after drinking our favorite holiday cocktail? Weren't we just giggling in the car with excitement over the gifts we purchased? Didn't we just have our annual Christmas lunch together while going over everything we had purchased for the kids? Didn't I just hear him sing "O Holy Night" in the Christmas Eve service? Didn't we just have our first tree-trimming party—in December of 1987? It seems like last year.

I thought I was doing great. Just put the Christmas decorations where they always go. How hard is that? I'd invited my family over for roasted hot dogs and chili the previous weekend to help decorate the tree. I thought the activity in the house would help. It did the opposite. I felt lonelier, like an outsider in my own home. I wanted to disappear into a dark closet. I went to my room to cry and ran into Mia doing the same thing. We hugged and cried together.

I told everyone I was ditching the idea of decorating the tree that night. I'd wait until it was only the kids and I. Everyone understood, except my little niece and nephews. I let them hang a few ornaments so they would think they'd helped. One by one, I pulled out some from the box that held my and Michael's ornaments. The children ran to me for each ornament without knowing that I continually swallowed a huge lump in my throat, as every ornament had a memory. I began disappearing inside the box.

Most of the ornaments were from our first tree-trimming

party, and the rest we collected each year from our travels. I kept searching for ornaments having no sentimental value. I couldn't bring myself to hand the children the ones that held precious personal memories, like the nest with two ceramic lovebirds in it that clips to a branch, or the one with wooden stockings hanging across a fireplace with all our names on it, or the wooden ones Michael painted as a child, or the little red elf that sat on a branch in the tree each year, often holding a special gift from him on Christmas morning.

As I handed the ornaments to my niece and nephews, my thoughts swirled in my head: *Is he really not in the next room drinking eggnog, laughing, and telling stories? Where did he go? Is he coming back? Am I the sole parent carrying on all of these traditions? Is my wedding ring really in a box now? This is really hard! Why does that lump come up so hard and suddenly in my throat? How can I breathe fine one minute and the next minute I can't catch my breath?*

We conquered one day at a time, one event at a time, one season at a time.

Be still and still moving.

I meet a woman who lost her husband ten years ago. After all these years, she still sees men from behind or at a distance who resemble him. It catches her breath and she actually thinks, *Oh, there he is!* She also still dreams about him in her sleep.

As she tells me these things, my eyes blur, lump bulging in my throat.

After almost a year, I have not had a "Michael spotting," and he's not been in my dreams. I've longed for a dream with him in it, any little dream—a glimpse of him in living motion. I've had none. Why is that? I thought I would dream about him often in my sleep, but, for whatever reason, I've not. Tonight my heart feels heavier when I get into bed. I ask God for a dream with Michael in it: *Lord, I just want to see his face.*

He gives me a dream.

I'm in my house; it's daytime. Two little African American boys are dropped off at my house to play for the afternoon. Once the boys are inside, I run outside to say something to their father before he drives away in his Suburban. I see the man in the driver's seat. His face is that of a man with whom I go to church. Running barefoot outside to catch him, I look down and realize I'm walking through a rose garden but it's pruned down to the ground. It's full of stubby, thorny branches with some random remainders of roses and their petals. I keep my head down as I tiptoe through the brambly bed of roses so I don't hurt my feet as badly. My face feels stressed, twisted up and burdened. To help me see more clearly, I hold my long hair back on one side as I look down. I notice that the dad in the car opens the door and steps outside. I look up: it's Michael. I feel shock come over me. He emerges with a big, happy grin on his face. His nose even wrinkles. He walks boldly and happily toward me with a smile. He looks just as he did the month he died. He's wearing a pair of flat-front khaki pants, a white dress shirt, and his current glasses. I feel the stress on my face lift away. My face feels lighter, as if I've been carrying a burden of weight on it. As it lifts from my face, my stressed face turns into a smiling face. I feel light-headed; I'm about to faint. As I watch him stride toward me, he changes to the Michael from the early nineties. His hair is longer in the back, his wire-rimmed glasses are larger, his shirt is still white but is a flowing, poet-like shirt. His pants are pleated and baggy instead of straight. Never breaking his stride, he comes happily toward me. We don't speak a word. Keeping his eyes on me, he smiles the whole time. I smile back in shock as I freeze among the brambly, stubby roses. Overcome with the moment, I black out, collapsing right into the thorny wasteland. I feel his hands come under my head and neck; he kisses me. I open my eyes, and all I see are his big blue eyes right in front of my face. We hold the gaze for a few seconds, then I wake.

I'm thankful for my encounter with Michael, but at the same time it's hard for me. Maybe God has been protecting my heart by keeping him from my dreams. For several weeks since the dream, I cry simply remembering it, seeing his smile and strength coming toward me. Three things about the dream stand out strongly: the weight of the burden I carried on my face, the feeling of it lifting, and the joy all over Michael's countenance. He comforted me in that dream by simply coming to me. He let me know he was well and whole.

I haven't had a dream about him since, nor have I asked God for one. One morning, the smell of his breath and the sound of his voice saying "Babe" woke me up in the early morning hours. I can't explain that.

All of this reminds me of something my friend Sally mailed me a couple months after Michael died. It's a quote from a book titled *In Lieu of Flowers*. Henry Scott Holland, a professor of divinity at Oxford University, wrote this quote within the book a century ago:

Death is nothing at all—I have only slipped away into the next room. I am I, and you are you. Whatever we were to each other, that we still are. Call me by my old familiar name, speak to me in the easy way you always used. Wear no forced air of solemnity or sorrow. Laugh at the little jokes we enjoyed together. Play, smile, think of me, pray for me. Let my name be ever the household word that it always was. Let it be spoken without the ghost of a shadow on it. Life means all that it ever meant...there is absolutely unbroken continuity. I am waiting for you— somewhere near, just around the corner. All is well.

Not long after the dream, I have a "Michael spotting."

Of course it doesn't make sense. I know I can't simply run into him. But all things familiar line up, and it feels real for one split second. The kids walk in front of me as we exit the church sanctuary. We approach a door leading to a back hallway; it pulls back quickly from the other side. A man holds it open for us to walk through before he enters the sanctuary. I don't pay any attention to who it is, but then glance in his direction as I approach the door. My heart flips, my body instantly radiates with heat, and I'm unaware of everything going on around me. My eyes brim with tears, which I had successfully held at bay throughout the entire service for the first time. At first glance, I don't even see his face, which is why I think it's Michael. His outfit is put together like Michael's would have been, his height is similar, and he stands patiently and happily as he allows my whole family through the door—just like Michael would have done. I look away quickly but then immediately glance back at him in an attempt to ground myself. I look into his face and give a faint smile. How did that just happen? How did my emotions respond so quickly as I thought he might be standing right before me? I know he can't be here holding the door open for me at church as he always did. Why did I immediately see this man as him?

All of this—the encounter, the shock, the tears, and the attempt to pull myself together—happens in a matter of seconds. The kids walk in front of me, and I struggle my way down the hall. My eyes focus straight ahead. I tune out everything and completely concentrate on pulling myself out of the emotional quicksand. I don't want the tears to spill out of my blurring eyes. (I've learned if I focus hard enough, I can force the tears to recede back from where they so quickly came.) I feel like I'm walking down a hallway in Willy Wonka's Chocolate Factory. The walls feel as if they are closing in on me. I'm disoriented and confused. This came out of nowhere— and within seconds I'll emerge from this hallway and be surrounded by people getting coffee. I have to get my wits back together as fast as I lost them. I'm not ready to handle more uncomfortable glances of sympathy. I choose to suck it up and push through the moment. I choke out a few good mornings, and then run into Craig—I'm safe. Unaware of what has happened, he small-talks about Emma Claire. It pulls me quickly back into this present moment.

The emotions that stir and erupt in a matter of seconds are astounding. They still blindside me without any forewarning. The wave hits, knocks the wind out of me. I stumble, sometimes fall to my knees in the rushing water, but then I struggle back to my feet and force one foot in front of the other—with deliberation and focus. It's an emotional workout that builds strength, ever so slightly, with each hit the waves take at me.

I look for some medicine in the medicine basket for Michael Anthony. He has a bad stuffy nose. I haven't put my hands in this basket for a year. I see all of Michael's old prescription meds from past sinus infections or back pain, for the occasional times he threw out his back just putting on socks. It hits me again how fast the year has passed. I can't believe I haven't thrown these away yet. This leads to my next thought: *There are so many things like this I still have not done.*

I've dealt with other, more pressing issues. Managing day-to-day living and survival, tying up all of Michael's business dealings. Then I am to try to clean out and purge stuff from my missing spouse? The purging easily became something at the bottom of the list. Looking at these old medicine bottles, I see how fleeting life and time truly are. These little things don't really matter in the big picture. At the same time, I can't help but think of the things I haven't done or finished this year. I try not to dwell on it too long.

Be still and still moving.

As I talk on the phone with Nanette, she reminds me of everything I *did* do this year. I'm usually not one to care what other people think, but if I'm honest with myself right now, I feel as if people look at what I haven't done and think, *I can't believe she hasn't done that yet.* I can't believe she hasn't cleaned that up yet. I can't believe she hasn't organized that yet. I can't believe that same stack of papers is still there. Is she ever going to go through those boxes in the corner? I do a little every day, but it's like pulling weeds. I pull the most unsightly ones first and then begin working on the others, one area at a time. By the time I get to the last area, there are more to pull where I started.

Things I still have not done:

Cleaned out his basket under his side of the sink with all
of his colognes and favorite hair products.
Cleaned out his brown leather Dopp kit.
Thrown away any of his prescriptions from our
medicine basket.
Finished thank-you notes for gifts or memoriam gifts
given in the second half of the year.
Found a new home for all of his high-end electric tools.
Finished going through his library of architecture books
that are still in boxes.
Enjoyed my garden.

The list of what I have done is longer; the intangible, even longer. I keep my focus on this list. With God's grace in abundance, I did these things:

I held my family unit together.
I ran toward God, not from Him.
I studied my children and learned even more about them.
I got out of bed every single day.

I did the next thing—each and every day.

I took the healing process very seriously, because it is serious.

I thanked God in the middle of it for the little things
    and the big.

I continued loving my children.

I was present for my children.

I prayed for my children.

Michael used to tell me, "Babe, if all you ever do is feed all of the children, and meet their needs, you have done enough." I think he told me that for such a time as this. I picture him saying that to me from across the dinner table at the end of a long day. He encouraged me and lifted me up out of my I-haven't-accomplished-anything-today mentality. I choose encouragement again.

Here it is: the one-year anniversary of Michael's death, home going, or departure, which are all of the different ways people have referred to his death. I dislike using the term *anniversary*. It usually means something celebratory, like our twenty-fifth wedding anniversary we would have celebrated this year, or the one-year anniversary of his business merger and new partnership we would have celebrated last month. This is an anniversary I have not looked forward to experiencing in any way.

The memories and details of that week are still fresh, and writing still brings me peace. I'm stronger from rising after each crashing wave. I feel empowered simply knowing I *am* walking. I choose to walk. I walk for Michael, for our children, for our future he helped build. The extent to which we are meeting each day's obstacles face-to-face, to which my children are strong and idealistic and compassionate young people, is an encouragement to me that God truly is sustaining us. Isaiah 40:29–31 has proven true in our lives:

> He gives strength to the weary
> and increases the power of the weak.
> Even youths grow tired and weary,
> and young men stumble and fall;
> but those who hope in the LORD
> will renew their strength.
> They will soar on wings like eagles;
> they will run and not grow weary,
> they will walk and not be faint. (NIV)

My faith continues to reemerge and gain momentum. Hope is rising. I remind myself the valley is not our destination. Psalm 23:4 says we only "walk *through* the valley of the shadow of death" (NKJV). Daily I choose not to make it my dwelling place. My hope comes in knowing that one day we *will* emerge out of the valley and dwell in safe pastures. The pastures are finally coming into view, far in the distance. With each passing day, my hands grip firmly to the hope in Psalm 23:6: "Surely goodness and mercy shall follow me all the days of my life; and I will dwell in the house of the LORD forever" (NKJV).

It's been difficult to focus on the "done" and the "goodness," to walk forward with strength, because at the same time, and in some ways, my very survival feels almost disloyal. Since Michael's death, I sometimes feel I need to stay in that place where everything seems suspended, neutral, frozen; where time stands still. The more days that pass, the farther I leave him behind. It's as if we're walking down a road and he stops. At first I stop with him. But I have to keep walking; life demands it. He just stands there, and though I don't want the distance between us to get any greater, I know the kids and I must keep walking. Even though the distance felt safe in the beginning, it's now an empty, lost feeling to walk forward without him. I keep looking back, confirming that he's not coming with us. But I do as T. S. Eliot says to do: "Be still and still moving...In my end is my beginning."

~ CHAPTER 11

Intentional Wandering

Not all those who wander are lost.

—J. R. R. TOLKIEN, *THE LORD OF THE RINGS*

Courage is fear that has said its prayers.

—KARLE WILSON BAKER, "COURAGE"

I FEEL AS IF OUR healing process is stuck. We have come far from where we started eighteen months ago, but now it seems as if we're not progressing any further. Mia made the same observation. I believe our restoration and healing have gone as far as they can in this town, this house, this place where Michael is everywhere, this place where everyone seems to know our story, this place where everyone knew Michael Barranco. We are in a fishbowl for everyone to observe. There's sympathy everywhere. Sympathy begins to feel like pity instead of empathy. A dark cloud hangs over us everywhere we go. It's difficult coming out from under it. If I stay home too much, people say I should get out, and if I get out with a smile on my face, people think I'm not grieving anymore or maybe I've moved on—or moved on too fast.

158

We need a change of scenery.

In *The Fellowship of the Ring,* one of Michael's and my favorite books, J. R. R. Tolkien penned the popular phrase "Not
all those who wander are lost." It's written within a riddle re-
ferring to Aragorn's ascension to the throne:

All that is gold does not glitter,
Not all those who wander are lost;
The old that is strong does not wither,
Deep roots are not reached by the frost.
From the ashes a fire shall be woken,
A light from the shadows shall spring;
Renewed shall be blade that was broken,
The crownless again shall be king.

The well-known second line refers to Aragorn's travels. He
is part of a group called the Rangers who are viewed as wan-
derers by those they protect from evil. They appear to wander,
but they are not lost. They are on a continual mission. *Wander*
usually means to move about aimlessly, to drift or stray. But as
Tolkien uses the word, it implies something completely different: to follow or pursue a winding course, to chase, go after
the winding. A wanderer can be a person who takes risks, an
explorer, a trailblazer, a pathfinder, or a pioneer. It's one who
makes a purposeful decision to wander. This is far from aimless.

Years ago, I gave Michael a T-shirt with NOT ALL WHO WAN-
DER ARE LOST printed across the front. He was headed off to
the mountains in Colorado for a spiritual "boot camp" given
by Ransomed Heart Ministries with John Eldredge. The shirt

had an image of a pair of hiking boots under the quote. You need a good pair of walking boots in order to go down all the roads where life may lead, if we allow it to guide us and if we trust it enough to wander with it. I also gave him a wristband with a small compass attached as a symbol for keeping his life, his wanderings, his priorities, and his goals heading in the right direction. He chose purposeful wandering while chasing after God. He took the risks that come with wandering. He was never lost. Every step had a purpose. He was on a mission.

I must now wander, take the risks that come with chasing after God.

Even though I felt lost when Michael died, my time alone with God makes me realize I am not lost but rather on a solitary mission to rediscover life, regain strength, and clarify my purpose. Wandering is not usually done in crowds or even in small groups. It's typically a journey of one. Maybe this journey will leave a trail for others to follow as God guides us to the other side of the Midnight Hour. I find myself on a dark and winding course, but I know my purpose can rise only if I follow closely behind Him—and so I wander with intention. This intentional wandering propels me with a sharper aim once I discover the path I'm destined to blaze. Jesus wandered in the desert before launching ahead into His life's purpose, but His wandering was far from aimless. As the Holy Spirit led Him, I hope He will also lead me.

Michael gave me a card a couple of years ago for no particular occasion. I discover it in my nightstand drawer. The front has words attributed to Ralph Waldo Emerson: "Do not go where the path may lead, go instead where there is no path and leave a trail. Always do what you are afraid to do. Be an opener of doors." When I read what Michael wrote on the inside, my stomach turns upside down:

"My prayer is that these trails will become roads for our children as they grow. That as they travel them, they too (as God directs) will venture off, creating trails of their own." I feel like this message is for such a time as this.

After much soul-searching and prayer, we move to New York State, from the Deep South of Jackson, Mississippi, to the heart of the Northeast in the Hudson River Valley. From southern accents, family, neighbors, lifetime friends, sweet tea and grits, and a familiar culture, to rural countryside, no connections, no family, no friends—and no sweet tea. I can't even find black-eyed peas or grits in the grocery store. The change is difficult but necessary.

I occasionally take the kids out by themselves on dates like Michael and I used to do. The idea of a move had been stirring inside of me. As I take each child out for dinner, I ask him or her the same question: "If we could live wherever you wanted to live, what places would be in your top three?" All three of them chose places with a big city or a country in Europe. New York was an overlap for all three. They had no idea why I asked this question, but I put the answer up on a shelf in my mind for more prayer. I waited for God to show me where and when He wanted us to move.

New York was the first answer He showed me. A rural setting that is close to New York City was the next direction. I look at homes located less than two hours from the city. I find what I think is the perfect house. I fly to the quaint little village in Dutchess County to see the house, along with some others the real estate agent has chosen. None of them, including the one that brought me here, is "the" house. I always loved older homes, antiques, high ceilings, and wooden floors, and usually loved homes that needed some TLC. Before flying to New York, I told God I wanted only the house He chose for us—no matter how different it looks. We needed a change.

At the last minute, the real estate agent offers to show me a house that can possibly work. He says, "It's not like any of the other ones we've shown you and doesn't have the number of bedrooms you want, but you could possibly make it work." We pull up a long driveway in the country to a late-1970s ranch-style home—I have never liked ranch-style homes. I step out of the car and feel God's presence. My body radiates with heat; the lump appears in my throat. We walk in the front door into a great room with vaulted ceilings everywhere. My real estate agent talks, but I can't hear a word he's saying. I gaze through the floor-to-ceiling windows that are everywhere I turn. The emotion builds—I can't stand the weight any longer. I excuse myself and run back to the driveway. Tears overtake me.

I'm shopping for a house for my family as a single parent, making a decision for our future without Michael while simultaneously hearing God say, "This is the one."

Back inside I tour the rest of the house, but in my heart it's already settled. This is our new home. Three months later, my five-thousand-square-foot home is purged and packed on an eighteen-wheeler. All the kids are excited about the new adventure.

I haven't lost my focus in life, but rather I realize it's time to pull off the main road. I take a different path because there seems to be a heightened significance in each step. Extreme focus is needed to stay the course. As a pioneer or an explorer searches for a path to follow, it may appear that he or she is lost, but that seeker is actually on a purposeful search, a mission to discover. I am that pioneer, on a mission to follow God at all costs. Our lives and our future depend on it.

My actions may look aimless, but they are far from it. I purposefully decide to follow a wandering course with God. It's the bravest thing I've ever done—and the hardest thing for others to understand. When people ask, "Why move? Why New York?" I can't give a firm answer. Most of the time I simply say, "I don't know yet, but I know I'm going to find out." And every day I learn a little more about why God brought us here, to a home on ten acres nestled in deep woods within a little village in New York. Every time I look out the floor-to-ceiling windows, I feel the weight of grief lift a little bit more as I breathe in nothing but nature—the trees, the mountains, the sunrises, the sunsets, the wild turkeys, the deer, the change of seasons in the woods, the owl that calls to me at night, the full moon lighting up the country sky, the hush after a heavy snow. Each time I take in the beauty, I feel as if God is saying, "This is why I brought you here. Breathe."

It reminds me of Tolkien's Rivendell, a beautiful, protected, hidden refuge in the misty mountains where Frodo Baggins and his unlikely band of companions pull away to rest, gain counsel, build strength and courage, and plan for the future. The beauty of God's creation and the peaceful calm surrounding us while hidden in the countryside of the Hudson River

Valley are a healing balm to every ounce of my being. My hidden refuge is a constant reminder that He *is* with us.

We have room here for emerging new emotions. We recognize and deal with our pains head-on. God's voice is easier to discern. It's easier because He pulled us back and placed us in a new town that forced the children and me to lean completely on Him and one another, without the distractions that came from all the familiar things back in Mississippi. We must drift alone for a season, away from the familiar, in order to gain deep, pure strength.

I chose to pull away from the noise and wander with God on this road to heal our wounded hearts and restore our lives. It's a refreshing change. Refreshing to have a clean start, to be in an entirely new and different place. Refreshing to walk without the feeling of dark clouds hanging over us. Refreshing that absolutely no one knows our story.

This wandering with God on an unchartered path serves another purpose: it adds a new dimension to my grieving process. It helps me find a way to move forward without feeling guilty; guilty because as I move on, I also leave my grief behind. I give myself permission to wander with God as my lead. I trust Him as we walk through the wilderness and toward the plans He has for our lives that lie ahead of us.

I still experience the waves of grief that often sweep over me. I am still walking through the Midnight Hour. I am still making sense of my life as a single parent and discovering who Jené Barranco is without Michael Barranco. But now I am also intimately in touch with God because of His intense guidance. I talk to Him constantly in the silent times throughout my day. Everywhere I look I see His presence. The closer I walk to

Him, the greater the courage I possess. God is taking the fear of the unknown during our wandering and molding it into the courage we need to press into and through the darkness.

It seems that everywhere I go, someone tells me how courageous I am. I tell them I don't feel courageous at all. I only do the next thing. I keep walking, one step at a time, with unaware courage. Without even realizing it, I'm living out the verse from Proverbs that has sustained me ever since the children were young: "Let your eyes look directly ahead [toward the path of moral courage] and let your gaze be fixed straight in front of you [toward the path of integrity]" (Prov. 4:25 AMP).

As Karle Wilson Baker says in her poem, "Courage is fear that has said its prayers." I learn courage does not necessarily mean there is an absence of fear. It is a boldness that rises higher than the fear. Boldness overpowers the fear *because* of the prayers. At times this boldness feels supernatural. It's as if God has placed blinders on me to help me plow straight ahead without slowing down. It's easy to lose courage if I look beside me, too far ahead of me, or even back from where I came. Courage rises only because I keep my eyes straight ahead.

Wholehearted obedience, or wandering with God, is by no means the easy road. Rick Warren says in *What on Earth Am I Here For?*, "It will sometimes be inconvenient, unpopular, cost me, doing the exact opposite of what our natural inclinations are." My move to New York is all these things, yet I know it's something God showed me I must do. It is a path I *had* to take. Why would I want to do something this hard of my own will, especially after what I've just been through? Does it make sense? Do I understand it? Do other people understand it? Is it convenient? #%*# no! Does it cost (and not just monetarily)? Have I lost relationships? Is it the exact opposite of what I want to do in the natural? Has it forced me out onto a limb? #%*# yes! But I feel safer in the middle of this dark, uncertain time while in God's perfect will and closely by His side than I would feel in the "comfortable" life floating down the road in Mississippi, which makes more sense to everyone else.

I've always pursued God's will in all situations in my life. Every morning, before I even get out of my bed to get coffee, I pray in God's will and His kingdom power for that day. I began this habit over twenty years ago. I've learned that following Him closely sometimes makes me unpopular. When people can't rationalize the decisions of others, it makes them uncomfortable and sometimes, in the worst case, judgmental. Even though I don't understand and can't even see the big picture, I'm willing to sacrifice all these things in order to follow God.

As my mom often says in an exasperated way when she doesn't understand the situation or know what she should do, "Just point me in the right direction" or "Just tell me what to do." This means "I can't do it on my own. You understand it and it's good enough for me." This is what God wants from me. This is what pleases Him. It's complete surrender. Others may look at it as foolishness or lack of wisdom if I move forward without a clear explanation or understanding. God looks at it as strength and courage and honoring Him— and it pleases Him. He is the one I choose to please.

Trust is a big thing for me since Michael died. In the physical world, I must discern when to trust or not trust people on a whole new level. Some workmen have tried to take advantage of the fact that I'm a woman, assuming I won't know any better if they do their job below standard or try to charge me more than they should. I learned to ask well-chosen questions, with a particular vocabulary. From the beginning of a job, I watch my words so the workman knows up front that nothing is getting past me regarding the work, the materials, or the billing. It's quite the opposite in the spiritual world.

With God I must completely, 100 percent, without a doubt, without hesitation, trust Him with every detail in my life. He is the only one watching my back 24/7. He is the only one who knows where my road leads. He is the only one who protects me, takes pleasure in me, and provides for me. My complete trust in Him has been the foundation for survival in every moment and every breath I've taken since Michael died. I trusted in God before, but at the same time, I trusted Michael for things in which I must now trust God. God says, "I want you to trust me in your times of trouble, so I can rescue you and you can give me glory" (Ps. 50:15 TLB). If I trust completely, even when I don't understand, He *will* rescue me.

I look to the Scriptures for someone who went out on a limb trusting God. Someone who had to do something inconvenient, something that made him or her unpopular. Someone who followed God on a path where there wasn't a trail. I gain strength studying someone who has gone before me. Noah is this person. He put trust and obedience together. "By faith, Noah built a ship in the middle of dry land. He was warned about something he couldn't see, and acted on what he was told. The result? His family was saved. His act of faith drew a sharp line between the evil of the unbelieving world and the rightness of the believing world. As a result, Noah became intimate with God" (Heb. 11:7 MSG).

I love the way this is worded in the Message version: "His act of faith drew a sharp line between..." His faith, his trust, set him apart from the ways of this world and placed him over on the side to accomplish God's purposes. I want to accomplish God's purpose for my life as Noah did. He trusted that God knew the bigger picture when He instructed him to build a boat the size of a football field on dry land, far away from any body of water, while anticipating rain, which up to this point in history had not fallen from the sky. *This* is trust without understanding.

I take this process of trusting and following His lead very seriously. I never want to miss it or, even worse, hear and see His lead but then choose not to take it. One day I may look back and think, *Ahhh, so that is why I had to do that!* But then again, I may never figure it out. I choose to wander with God, forgoing understanding. I trust Him—even during what feels like the "ministry of absence."

I find myself frequently answering a question asked by many people: "So how was it?" They are asking about something I experience that was emotionally difficult for me. My short response is "It was hard but good." When I say this, I mean it was a difficult experience for me to walk through, but it was good for me to press through and do it anyway. Sometimes it's hard and not good—it's hard but I feel like I didn't gain any strength, courage, or release of pain from having to do it.

Writing my blog is hard for me as I gather all my feelings, put words to them, and then cry as I experience them again while I read my words, but it's good for my emotional state to get those feelings out of my heart and mind. Sending Michael Anthony off for four weeks of camp the summer after Michael died was hard for both of us, but good for building his self-confidence and helping him rely on his inner strength. Going to the beach for the first time without Michael was hard, but good for our health and our time of bonding as a new family unit. The children's piano recital was hard, but good because strength and confidence grew in their hearts from overcoming such great obstacles. Going to the cemetery for the first time by myself was hard, but a good time of solitude, talking to God, and crying for Michael.

Our move to New York was a huge hard but good.

Attending all of the business meetings with attorneys and financial people was hard, and not good. They are reminders that Michael is no longer a part of this arrangement and I'm trudging through all of these decisions alone. Moving everything out of Michael's office was hard, and not good. Going to church without him was hard, and not always good. Choosing a headstone and bench for the cemetery—this was hard, not good.

Some things are hard but build character, or at least I can see what I will learn when I get to the other side. At other times, things are plain hard and I can't see the good in them. Most things during the first year were plain hard; making simple daily decisions was hard. There are many more things I'll continue to experience that will be hard. Will they be good for me, too? I don't know. There is always more to learn, more room to grow, more room to heal. I still take things one day at a time—even a half a day at a time.

Even with the time that has passed, I keep experiencing the hard but good. The hard-but-not-good experiences are spreading farther and farther apart. Our first Thanksgiving in New York is hard but good. My mom and dad come up, and we create a whole new holiday experience. Thanks to my cheer-coaching background and friends in the business, the kids and I are on the Spirit of America float in the Macy's Thanksgiving Day Parade. We go to a local Christmas tree farm and choose our tree in freezing temperatures. We watch our first Thanksgiving snow. We build the first fire of the season and fill the house with smoke because we don't open the flue. Michael Anthony goes to "real" school in Connecticut, Indian Mountain School. His first day is hard because it's a "first," but good because we see it as a wonderful adventure for him as he experiences a whole new world. He meets new friends from all over the world. He flows into a wonderful music program. This is all hard but really good.

Wandering with God is hard but good.

In *What on Earth Am I Here For?*, Rick Warren proposes three of life's greatest questions: the question of existence, the question of significance, and the question of intention. To my remembrance, I've never struggled with these questions in my entire life. I've always known there is a reason for my existence, my life matters, and there is a purpose for my life. But since I lost Michael, my life, my journey, my purpose, have detoured. I can no longer recognize my purpose as I once did.

A detour doesn't mean my purpose changed. It means only

an altered trajectory, not a new purpose. While married to Michael, my purpose outside of being a mother to my children and a wife to Michael Barranco had become obscured from my vision. When Michael died, my purpose as his helpmate on our journey as man and wife, parents, and followers in Christ was altered by his absence. But the purpose God planned for my life hasn't changed solely because Michael is no longer with me on the journey. I've stumbled using my new map on this journey. I was comfortable with the old map. I've begun personifying purpose during my search. Physically, she looks different now, but she's still the same purpose. I look at her every day, trying to recognize the new face she has.

When someone has had a terrible accident and completely damages his face, he has reconstructive surgery and scars. Sometimes the damage is so severe that his close friends may look at him and think, *Is that you? You look so different.* It's even uncomfortable being around him at first because things feel different than they once did. Eventually, familiarity is restored. Since Michael died, I feel as if I'm squinting while looking at the purpose God has had for me since the beginning of time, straining my eyes to see something familiar. In my mind I think, *Is that you, Purpose? How will you look without Michael by my side? How will you manifest yourself now that the surroundings and the people have changed?*

This is where I struggle.

I know the significance is there. I know there is still a purpose for my life, but I feel as if I've been given a new owner's manual to teach me a different way to use a tool I've had my whole life. A tool I used so much it was comfortable in my hand, a natural extension of my body. I'm not comfortable with Purpose right now. She became so intertwined with Michael's purpose that it's strange to see her separate from his. She and I are getting reacquainted. We're trying to get past the awkward moments. I recognize her face more and more with each passing day as she wanders alongside me. Every once in a while, a situation arises or a conversation takes place with someone new, and suddenly I catch a glimpse of her, in a new location. I almost feel my heart say, "There you are! I have missed seeing you."

Rediscovering my purpose has been hard but good.

For such a time as this—it echoes repeatedly in my head since Michael died. Mordecai speaks these words to Esther, his adopted orphaned cousin. "Yet who knows whether you have come to the kingdom for *such* a time as this?" (Esther 4:14 NKJV).

Her sole purpose may be for this very moment in time—brought to this place, this time, to be the catalyst to save her people, the Jewish nation. If she's silent, choosing not to appeal to the king on behalf of the Jews, she may miss the opportunity, the purpose, for where God has placed her.

For such a time as this means being situated in the right place, doing the right thing, surrounded with the right people, to make a difference at the right time.

As homeschool parents, we were, of course, often asked why we chose to do this. In the beginning, we gave our list of detailed reasons. We soon realized the main reason was the only one that mattered: we believed it was what God wanted for our lives. *He* chose it for us. And so we followed Him. We desired His perfect will in all areas of our lives, even if it meant homeschooling our children, going against the mainstream. I received my degree in education, which didn't make sense to me at the time, but it was for such a time as this. It was hard but good.

The kids are gifted, musically talented, highly social, and a joy to be around. Because I've spent so much one-on-one time with them, we communicate honestly together. Needs are expressed or typically noticed. Our relationship has been priceless—for such a time as this. Because they were homeschooled, they were able to rest and pull away for as much time as they needed after losing their father. Their musical abilities have been great therapy for them. There has been much guitar playing, drumming, piano playing, and singing. Ten years of music and twelve years of homeschooling—for such a time as this.

We lived in a beautiful neighborhood with a close-knit community. We moved into that home in 1999. I always told Michael there wasn't any place in Jackson I'd rather live. If we ever moved, it would be to the country for bigger pets, bigger gardens, and bigger sunsets. For several years before he died, we desired to move to the country, but the timing never felt right. Imagine if I had been in the country when I lost Michael, without neighbors checking on me or helping me at a moment's notice? We were placed in that neighborhood—for such a time as this.

I discovered I loved writing during a creative writing course my senior year at Woodland Hills Baptist Academy. It took me by surprise. I always loved to draw but had never even written in a journal. After Michael and I married, the writing came out in full force; we wrote our feelings for each other in multiple ways. In the 1990s, God showed me the need to develop my writing in any form on a daily basis. Finding the time was difficult, but I became aware of it and used it as a creative outlet. I didn't understand the purpose of where God was taking it, but now I'm thankful for the written gift. Writing helps me feel, understand, and grieve—for such a time as this.

"To everything there is a season and a time for every matter *or* purpose under heaven" (Eccles. 3:1 AMPC). I see my purpose as being akin to a rudder on a boat moving me with direction and force. I know she's always been there. She hasn't changed; she only gradually turned me with each changing season of life. Looking back, I see where I've led and inspired people in different ways: parenting, teaching, ministering, homeschooling, coaching, choreographing, and mentoring. But now, without planning it or seeing it coming, this lifelong purpose of inspiring and teaching others is funneling into leading and helping others through my writing about my grief journey. I want others to see that they can come out strong and alive on the other side of the dark valley, face the fears, and overcome the pain and confusion and watch courage rise, as I'm still doing.

The success of my role in life, even my very survival, depends entirely on my unity with God's will as I wander with Him—for such a time as this.

I love gardening. I love digging my fingers in dirt. I love the smell of wet soil. I love choosing what colors and textures of plants will look good together. I love a beautiful flowerbed. I love watching a collection of pots with plants spilling over the edge come together like a tantalizing meal. I love gardening with someone. I love gardening alone. I love the sound of the pebble paths connecting garden spaces under my feet. I love pruning. I love roses—all kinds. I love peonies, hydrangeas, herbs, Louisiana irises, Shasta daisies, English aster, wisteria, Carolina jasmine, and confederate jasmine. I love deadheading spent blooms. I love looking at a freshly mulched area. I even love weeding.

I love what each season brings.

In spring, I love seeing color emerge—I love watching perennials come back to life. I love trying something new in the garden. In summer, I love enjoying the fruit of my spring labors, the never-ending time of weeding, and eating seasonal fruits and vegetables. I love how autumn ushers in a feeling of a fresh start, just like spring. I love fall cleaning in the garden, the change of colors from bright to warmer shades, and the crunching of dry leaves underfoot. I love planting mums and new perennials, decorating with pumpkins, and smelling cinnamon and cider in the air. I love the starkness of the winter in the garden. I love seeing the horizon through the tall, skeletal trees. I love the unexpected majesty of the trees with absolutely nothing adorning them. I love the minimalist beauty of the garden in the winter. I love dreaming about what I will do the next spring.

"As long as the earth remains, there will be springtime and harvest, cold and heat, winter and summer, day and night"

(Gen. 8:22 TLB). The earth was created for seasons of change, and so were we. How tiresome and bland would life be if there were only spring, or only winter? In Mississippi, I found myself in what felt like a continual winter. My life needed a season change. It felt bland. Like a bear in the winter pulls away to hibernate and build strength, even my desire for gardening retreated into complete hibernation, as if in the dead of winter. I hope it awakes one day. My scenery needed changing to help usher in a new season.

In New York, I can at least see winter's end on the horizon—but it's still winter. It often feels cold and stark. I long for the spring, for the season of growth and new life. Despite the season I see outside my windows, I finally feel my season in life changing. I feel the Midnight Hour drawing to a close. The sunrise is slow, but I feel its warmth on my face as it peeks through the trees.

The changes of seasons are usually gradual in the garden and in our lives, but occasionally they happen suddenly. I experienced a seasonal change just as a cold snap kills all of your spring plants, or as an ice storm causes power loss, or a debilitating blizzard in the middle of the night brings life to a standstill. We were forced into a season of dormancy. I keep asking myself, *What can I learn in this season? Is there something I can enjoy? If I enjoy something in every season in the garden, what can I possibly enjoy in this season of my life?*

Ecclesiastes 11:8 says, "People ought to enjoy every day of their lives" (NCV), and in 1 Thessalonians 5:18, Paul says, "Give thanks in all circumstances; for this is God's will for you in Christ Jesus" (NIV). Really? Why do these Scriptures have to be in the Bible? Why couldn't they specify particular seasons for these to be true? The verses could tell us: During this season, keep your head in a hole; this season, play outside; that season, shut your door and don't come out until the storm is over. Paul kind of blew it for me when he said, "I have learned to be content whatever the circumstances." (And whatever the season.) In Philippians 4:11, Paul, having been a prisoner, been shipwrecked, had death threats against him, and experienced starvation, physical beatings, alienation—and the list goes on and on and on—says give thanks and be content (NIV)?

There must be something to enjoy in each season. The Scriptures wouldn't command us to "enjoy every day of [our] lives" if God is not simultaneously providing something for us to enjoy in every season. I *want* to enjoy my days. I *desire* it. Why can't I embrace each season and enjoy it as easily as I embrace the seasons in the garden? I know there's a purpose to every season. I must experience each one in order to appreciate the onset of the next. "There is a time for everything, and a season for every activity under the heavens" (Eccles. 3:1 NIV).

I fully embraced the winter but now am ready for a change. I had a subtle change when I chose to wander with God. Wandering is a season, too, just like it was for the Israelites. I wander after God as I slowly leave winter behind and edge into spring.

CHAPTER 12

False Spring

The more people I love, the more vulnerable I am.

—MADELEINE L'ENGLE, *TWO-PART INVENTION*

CONQUERING THE NIGHT WAS A SLOW, uphill battle. Restlessness or sleeplessness came around on most nights. More often than not, I made a trip to the bathroom during these times. I hated getting out of bed, because fear often caught my thoughts in the dark of the night, a constant reminder: *You're all alone.* Even passing the sink in my vanity area felt empty; it's just for me now. His usual remnants were no longer there. Each time I walked back to bed, I imagined him sleeping on his side. As I climbed into the empty bed, a wave of loneliness came over me. The silence enveloped me. I stared at his pillow while imagining his sleeping face—I tried to hear his breathing in my memory. After listening to the silence, I took a deep breath and rolled over. I wished it were time to get up for the day. The daylight hours have distractions, the activity of life. At night, it was my memories of Michael's presence, and yet I was alone.

In our home in New York, I notice a change. As I walk past my sink in the dark tonight, I feel different. I'm comfortable being alone at night. I've conquered the dark night. The sink and the vanity area have become mine; there is no longer a shadow lurking to stab my heart as I walk past. I approach my bed and look at his side. I recognize that a new normal has settled into my nighttime routine. The room is still painfully silent, but it doesn't feel empty—it's full of God's grace and me. I get into bed, glance at Michael's side, and feel the acceptance take place.

I watched the night continuum go from peaceful, restorative rest with loving silence next to my husband, to fear, terror, sleeplessness, painful silence, and loneliness, and now to a calm acceptance of being alone. God's peace is tangibly present through every minute of the night.

"He makes me lie down in green pastures, he leads me beside quiet waters, he refreshes my soul" (Ps. 23:2–3 NIV).

Even though I'm now at peace with my aloneness at night, the suffocating blanket of loneliness is present during many of my waking hours. I'm a continual student with an insatiable appetite to learn, grow, and transform while moving forward in life. Examining life with much introspection is a regular habit. Questions continually run through my head: *Why did I respond that way? Why did that change? Why don't I do that anymore? Why did I ever do that before? Why am I feeling this way? Why does that hurt my heart? Why did that make me cry? What does this mean? Why am I afraid of that? Why do I hold on to that?*

What am I supposed to learn from this? Why is grief still lingering so? Why do I feel so lonely all of the time?

This kind of questioning brings me to an epiphany: I have mistaken loneliness for grief.

It reminds me again of C. S. Lewis's words in *A Grief Observed*: "No one ever told me that grief felt so like fear. I am not afraid, but the sensation is like being afraid." No one ever told me that loneliness felt so like grief. I'm not grieving, but the sensation is like grief. The symptoms are almost identical; it's hard to discern one from the other. Grief is a lonely emotion, but loneliness is not grief. Loneliness is a close companion to grief and follows on its heels. It's one of my biggest enemies. No amount of resolve or prayer seems to keep loneliness away. It numbs me, just as fear and grief did in the beginning.

Our first Thanksgiving in New York brought us supernatural joy. Experiencing it with my parents made it feel like a wonderful vacation together. My parents had prayed hard for us in the weeks and months after Michael's death. And yet I felt the tragedy cut me off from them. It wasn't their fault. I felt cut off from everyone. Grief does this, and I was lonely. Grief is a process I had to endure alone. The children had to endure it alone, too, each of us internally processing in our own way.

But here in New York, as we spent time together with my parents, I felt that vital connection renewed. I remember my dad's joy while watching the first snowfall. He and Mom sat with their chairs turned toward the windows. He responded as if he were watching a fabulous fireworks show. They both grew up in Illinois, where it snowed, and then moved to Mississippi, where it didn't.

His reaction to the snowfall reminded me of his awe as he watched the Knicks and Celtics play in Madison Square Garden the spring before I moved to New York.

I had surprised him with a quick trip to New York with tickets to a Knicks game. They played the Boston Celtics, his favorite team. He'd played basketball in college and taught me how to shoot the perfect free throw when I was in the eighth grade. His nickname in college was Downtown Donny because he could swish a shot from "downtown," past the three-pointer line.

Our tickets were courtside. I'll never forget the awestruck look on his face as we stood watching both teams warm up before the game. He barely moved as he took in all the sights and sounds. After a few minutes of silence, he turned to me and with all sincerity said, "You don't ever have to get me another gift for the rest of my life."

At Thanksgiving last year, I remember how proud he was of our new home. He was proud of my courage to start over in a new place. When he and Mom left on the plane back to Mississippi, it marked some kind of watershed for me. With God's love, steadfast presence, and subtle guidance, we were making our way through the darkness. I was making my way out of grief and treading delicately through loneliness.

The first signs of spring emerged—but now, just as before, we experience another severe cold snap.

A harrowing case of the flu nails me. I've been in my bed for weeks. I feel alone and frightened without another adult in the house. I depend solely on the kids for my every need, and they do an amazing job. As instructed by the doctor, face masks hang on my doorknob for them to wear when they enter my room. The loneliness falls on me like a dense fog—then Julie calls me with the news.

Dad has had a severe stroke. I'm in my bed in New York during the third week of the flu while my dad is in a hospital bed in Mississippi, slipping in and out of consciousness. I can barely walk to the bathroom and can't make it down the hall to the kitchen. Getting on a plane and flying to his bedside is out of the question. For seven days, I live by text messages from my four siblings and conversations with my mom. I keep thinking, *If I can only get the strength to shower and walk to the kitchen, I can fly to Mississippi to hold his hand.*

I finally feel a little stronger. Julie calls again: he's transferring to hospice. I have four days, at best, to get there before he dies.

We fly on a cold and rainy Sunday afternoon. I hold his hand and throw myself across his chest as he lies there struggling to breathe with his eyes closed. I kiss his hands, his forehead, his cheeks. I caress his soft gray hair. I study our hands together and realize how similar they are. He is unresponsive but miraculously gives my hand a little squeeze. I hold a cool, damp cloth on his warm forehead. I whisper in his ear. I thank him for what he's been to me. I tell him he's done a great job. I pray aloud. I recite my favorite Scripture to him. I tell him I love him.

O God, You *are* my God;
early will I seek You;
my soul thirsts for You;
my flesh longs for You

in a dry and thirsty land
where there is no water.
So I have looked for You in the sanctuary,
to see Your power and Your glory.
Because Your loving kindness *is* better than life,
my lips shall praise You.
Thus I will bless You while I live;
I will lift up my hands in Your name.
My soul shall be satisfied as with marrow and fatness,
and my mouth shall praise *You* with joyful lips.
When I remember You on my bed,
I meditate on You in the *night* watches.
Because You have been my help,
therefore in the shadow of Your wings I will rejoice.
My soul follows close behind You;
Your right hand upholds me. (Psalm 63:1–8 NKJV)

A rare snowfall covers Jackson that night in a thick blanket. I awake the next morning as my cell phone rings. It's Julie's final call. Another kind of winter begins again.

I return to New York. A long stretch of months with new emotions begins. New because they are slightly different from the grief I felt when Michael died. I'm experiencing loneliness—loneliness in addition to grieving over my dad and loneliness for his presence. He was the other man in my life. I sat under his teaching of God's word as a child and an adult, when he was preaching and when he was not. He baptized me when I was in the third grade. He walked me through my spiritual questions in every stage of life. He looked me in the eyes and listened to me for however long I needed to talk. He built up my confidence in my writing; he discussed ideas with me on every paper I ever wrote in college. He taught me to laugh through *Looney Tunes* and *The Three Stooges*. His laugh was contagious. I long for a call from him with his voice on the other end saying, "What's cookin', good lookin'?" or "What's up, doc?"

I wander with God down another twist in this unchartered road. I'm aware I must now rebuild my sense of self, my purpose as the lone leader of my family, even as I let go of parts of my past. "Not only is there a season for every matter, but also a season for every purpose!" This verse from Ecclesiastes keeps reverberating in my mind over and over again. I think the end of a purpose is the hardest kind of season to put behind us— especially when we loved that purpose and we were loved by it in return. My season and purpose for being a daughter to my dad and a wife to Michael are over. These purposes invigorated me, inspired me, and made me feel secure while enveloped by them. I learned great things from those purposes. I grew because of them. They stirred my soul. But there *will* be another season; it's the way life works. God is remodeling my purpose. The structure and the foundation are the same, but He is re-purposing its use. Seasons and purposes build on one another.

I sit here looking back at all of this to extrapolate what I can, to learn from my questioning. There are times when looking back is a good thing if the purpose for looking back is to learn from my past to help improve my future. In keeping my eyes straight ahead on the road that lies before me, I must sometimes look back to recognize a pattern or where I experienced roadblocks, to know what worked and didn't work, or to remember where I made a wrong turn so I won't do it again. Looking back for the sole purpose of bemoaning what I see or wishing things had turned out differently doesn't help me. In fact, it can cause me to stumble over my feet if I turn around while walking forward at the same time.

, I look at photographs taken during the first few months in New York. I notice my face is lit up again with joy. The grief, the tiredness, the darkness, and the pain seem lifted from my countenance. I see hope in my eyes again. The spark was short-lived. For countless months I thought I was only grieving, but now I realize that the grieving had turned into sheer loneliness even before my dad died. I'm sad from being separated from someone who loves me for me. I'm lonely without anyone to share my life on a daily basis. It feels bleak, desolate—it's loneliness. Over two years of living inside my own little time capsule, pulled away from people, without my life companion beside me, and now experiencing the absence of the man who stood by me, encouraged me, and fought for me my entire life brings me to the doorstep of loneliness.

I wondered if I was ever going to come out of the deep grief, but now I realize I had—even if it only rolled over into a state of loneliness. The loneliness I feel means I'm ready and need to allow people back into my life. As I'm an introvert by nature, this will always have some limitations. But this is a positive step forward in this journey. It propels me even more toward my purpose. The step from grief over to loneliness is actually a good sign to me. Loneliness can be remedied; grief, death, loss cannot. Grief is what it is. Death is what it is.

It's part of the natural life cycle. It's at the end of the road for every living being. We live and then we die, and yet every time death appears, we feel stunned and dumbfounded that it's arrived at our doorstep. Why do we arrogantly and instinctively hold on to the thought that death will never come near to us, that it's something only other people experience?

Death is inescapable.

Yesterday I learned of the sudden death of the father of a friend of Mia's. The specific cause is unclear to me, but something like an aneurysm or seizure took his life. He'd just remarried a week ago, with all of his children participating in the wedding. The exuberant, newlywed bride is now instantaneously a widow. A week of life renewed, joy restored, immediately followed by an unannounced journey down a road of utter darkness, grief, and pain—with an unknown distance to travel before the sun rises again. The oppression on this road will at times cause her to crawl while gasping for air instead of walking upright with each unknown step toward living again.

This morning I learn that the college son of a woman in our village died instantly in a car accident on his way home last night. I have an image in my mind of him rising a little late yesterday morning, eating a leisurely breakfast, and discussing his day and plans with his parents, then enjoying his summer day before heading out last night with his friends. As he walks out the door, he turns to his mom and says, "I'll text you when I'm heading home." But instead of a text from her fully alive son, she receives a phone call or a personal visit from the authorities. So begins her journey of survival down the shadowy, incomprehensible road of grief: the Midnight Hour.

In an instant: full life and light, then death and darkness.

After hearing the news early this morning, I sit in my bed and weep. My stomach convulses. I weep for this mother. I weep for the newlywed bride. I weep for the other children involved. I want to hold them or sit silently next to them and allow them to cry, moan, scream, writhe, or whatever they need to do to let the initial pain escape. I hurt deeply as I see them in my imagination taking their first steps into the valley of the shadow of death. I see the fear on their faces as they anticipate the steps and the days to come on a road they have never traveled, on a road with no map, because it's a different journey for each person. They must only keep moving forward.

I yearn to help them carry the load. I yearn to open the skies above them so the suffocating air can be released. I yearn to go before them with a shield and blaze the trail for them, but it's something they must—we all must—experience alone. It's a singular journey. We can silently hold their hands, bring them provisions, and listen to their tales of the journey, but in the end, it's *their* journey.

We all inevitably embark on this path at some point in our lives. No amount of mental preparation can equip us for the onslaught of the pain, the memories, and the dark hours experienced on the journey. The only mental preparation I had before Michael died was my faith in God. It was the place from which I drew my strength and protection while traversing this path of sheer darkness. It was, and still is, my source of hope, my source of healing, and my source of peace when everything about me rages.

Today I glance behind me into the dark valley from which

I'm about to emerge. I can barely make out the silhouettes in the distance of these broken people as they drag themselves slowly and warily into the other end of this devastating valley. Lord, be with them. Hold them. Rescue them. Protect them. Cast a light for them:

> I am poured out like water
> and all My bones are out of joint;
> my heart is like wax;
> it has melted within me.
> My strength is dried up like a potsherd.
> and My tongue clings to My jaws;
> You have brought Me to the dust of death...
> But You, O Lord, do not be far from Me;
> O My Strength, hasten to help Me! (Psalm 22:14–15 and
> 19 NKJV)

Even with the kids in the house, the house often feels lifeless. No matter what we're doing, it's obvious that somebody and something is missing. When we sit down for a meal, we still feel the void in the room without Michael at the table with us. Even when he wasn't in the house physically, just the *idea* of him helped fill up the house with life and activity. Now it seems the whole day is full of silence. We retreat to our rooms at different times throughout any given day, each approaching and grappling the state of our hearts in different ways.

I learn I must practice proactively creating life in the house.

It keeps loneliness at bay. I know this revelation is from God because I don't believe I have the ability right now to make my brain work this way. In the past, we did certain things when company came over or when Michael came home at the end of the day. These actions created an expectancy of fellowship and a love for life itself. I bring these old habits back to life.

I play music on the iPod speakers in the late afternoons in the kitchen; it's a huge help. The kitchen is still the hub of all conversation and activity, and music brings life into the atmosphere and beauty into the moment. Sound, in general, creates life in the house. The sound of the dishwasher running proves we've been eating, living, and using our kitchen. I love the sound of the washing machine or dryer going through their cycles. Mondays were once laundry day, but now I throw in a load at any time. I feel productive, and it creates a sense of normalcy; life is going on. The act of cleaning the kitchen makes the atmosphere feel fresh and renewed. In the past, I made sweet mint tea or peach tea when company came over for a visit. Now I do it for *us* to enjoy—just because. Recently, Michael Anthony poured himself a big glass and said, "Mom, did you make this tea for anything special?" My reply was no, I'd made it for us to enjoy. He flashed a big smile and said, "Thanks!" I burn more scented candles. A lit candle not only is soothing with its flickering light and aroma, but also makes the room feel special—it says peace and conversations are welcome here. Inviting a friend over for a glass of wine, planning trips with the kids, or even organizing closets makes me feel as if life is in the house.

I'm finally cooking again—not at the same level I did before, but I'm getting a meal on the table and occasionally baking.

Home cooking brings life and anticipation of something good back into the house. It shows that someone lives here and loves it. I always loved cooking for my family and for company: the smells, the action in the kitchen, the conversations around the kitchen counter, the satisfaction of making something delicious for the people I love, and most importantly, the life it brought to the house. I have fresh blueberries right now, so I'm thinking about baking blueberry streusel muffins, Mia's favorite. Michael would moan with delight as I pulled them out of the oven. He came home from work if I baked. He enjoyed anything I baked while it was hot; he loved being there in the glory of the moment when everything was fresh and on the counter. He'd eat one of whatever I made, make some noise while closing his eyes, and then say, "Mmmmm! Oh, babe!"

Creating life in a home that has lost a precious life is hard. Sometimes it feels laborious and fake. Sometimes I simply walk around looking for ways to make the house feel alive. Once I do something, anything, a boost of life follows. All of these things I do seem small, but a beautiful life is built from an accumulation of many small acts. I've done it before and I'll do it again. I believe these small acts help the children and me feel all is well. They bring a feeling of security and stability. We are living our lives. God is the great Creator of life. I am made in His image. He's showing me how to create life and beauty in this broken, fallen world.

Just when I'm beginning to experience a calm after the storm, my kids begin walking through their own storms. New tsunamis strike them at staggering intervals. As tsunamis rise suddenly from the ocean's depth with life-threatening force, post-traumatic stress disorder also rises up from the deep, forcing its victims to hold on to life with every ounce of strength just to remain standing and breathing.

My place for prayer is no longer sitting in bed or in my writing chair. I'm on my knees or facedown on the floor while I cry to God for mercy. Now the daily fight is for the healing and protection of their hearts, minds, and bodies. I stand before them and help them wield strength and faith against the frequent attacks of PTSD.

Moods, stress levels, anxieties, lack of sleep, coping mechanisms, bad dreams—it's one long roller-coaster ride as each child rises and falls at different intervals. Mia braves the onslaught while she's solo off at college. She speaks with a counselor once a week, but juggling her studies along with her emotions keeps her on the edge. We have many phone calls with her crying on the other end. She's in basic survival mode.

Julia has multiple episodes of mentally checking out, with her eyes glazed and not responsive, and even toddler-like tantrums. Recently she passed out and remained unconscious for forty-five minutes. When she awoke she couldn't speak. For more than an hour she typed her words on her laptop for me to read. Sometimes she runs from the dinner table and throws herself facedown on her bed. When asked what's wrong, she says through her sobs, "I miss Dad!" She's finally crying, after three years of not shedding a tear.

Michael has outbursts of extreme anger. His thought processes are completely irrational. He's withdrawing and losing his gregariousness. This boy who was once "the mayor" of our neighborhood in Mississippi because of his ability to greet everyone and engage in conversation is now pulling back from his strengths. He runs away into the woods when he can't handle a situation. His grades have declined. He has difficulty falling asleep and then difficulty waking up in the morning.

I read Isaiah 43:1–3 again to stir my faith:

"Fear not, for I have redeemed you;
I have called you by name, you are mine.
When you pass through the waters, I will be with you;
and through the rivers, they shall not overwhelm you;
when you walk through fire you shall not be burned,
and the flame shall not consume you." (ESV)

He *will* walk with us through these circumstances. I'm banking on it.

I return from a five-day trip to Nashville with Julia for my niece's wedding and two college visits. While we're there, Mia and her best friend Anna Maria meet up with us. They're in the middle of a two-week road trip from Boston to Mississippi as a reward for their recent college graduations. Julia and I do the college visits alone for two of the days, then spend time with family for Frankie's wedding. This makes the second family wedding in three weeks, and we have two more to go over the next two weekends. In between the two weddings is Mia's graduation weekend.

Just when I thought most of the first experiences since

Michael's death were over, a steady succession of waves pounds me. My first family wedding to attend without Michael by my side: Julie ties the knot. Everyone encourages me to stand in line with the single women to catch the bouquet—which I do—and I catch it. Another first. My first child to graduate from college and Michael isn't beside me. My first official college visit as a single parent navigating the winding path to college for Julia. Each "first" these past three weeks hit me a little harder than the previous one.

With barely enough time to regroup my emotions from Julie's wedding, five days later I find myself sitting quietly alone in the back of a crowded chapel for Mia's baccalaureate service. Looking around, I see families and couples everywhere. I feel pride swelling in my heart as I think of the strength Mia found to go to college just five months after losing her father, of her strength not only to go, but also to finish. She did it. We did it. Homeschooled from kindergarten to twelfth grade, supported by Michael and me every step of the way—and here she is, finished.

The music plays, and a weight sinks in my chest. My eyes brim with tears, the tears of a different kind—my throat bloats with a lump. I sit motionless, absorbed in the moment.

Dear Jesus, keep holding this angel in Your hand! Call her Angel, just like her dad once did. Give her steady, warm encouragement, just like her dad always did. Restore her heart. Give her supernatural rest and restoration. You gave her such abundant grace for this! You did it! Guide her in Your way. Keep her heart tender to You. Reward her for her faithfulness. Don't take Your eyes off of her, God; she still needs You more than ever!

Four days later, I'm on a plane with Julia heading to Nashville for her college visits to Belmont University and Vanderbilt, then comes Frankie's wedding weekend.

After the wedding ceremony in Nashville, I hug Johnny, my brother-in-law, who has just given away his oldest daughter in marriage. I can't stop the hug. This is his first of two daughters to give away in marriage—and it's six years after Theresa's death from cancer. As I stand here embracing him, my heart aches. I feel my insides melting. I know he feels my void just as I feel his today. My heart aches for him. It aches for his girls. It aches for me. It aches for my kids as they begin testing their wings into young adulthood while still battling PTSD. My heart aches for the uncertainties ahead. More tears of a different kind roll down my cheeks.

These children seem to be slipping through my fingers as they quickly approach adulthood. Have I done all I can do? Did I let them down? Was I there when they needed me most? How are their hearts doing in all of this? Can we go back in time? Is this easier for them and harder for me? God, why has everything been so hard? When will the journey lighten up more? I'm just beginning to feel my heart heal from letting Michael go, but now I'm feeling a similar pain—this void as I let my kids go and watch them leave my nest. God, I feel more alone again as they venture ahead without me. But I want them to live, love, learn, and explore all that You have for them. Don't let go of us, God.

At home in New York again, I say good-bye to Julia as she leaves our home with every available inch of her car crammed with her belongings. My mom is her travel companion as they drive from New York to Mississippi, a two-day trip. Julia's coaching a swim team this summer and competing with her swimming again, after a three-year break. When we hug in the kitchen, it's like my hug with Johnny: I can't stop. I don't want to let her go. We both feel the ache in our hearts.

Her roller-coaster ride with PTSD this last year, as well as her continuing battle against an extreme case of Lyme disease she contracted last summer, has taken us on an emotionally exhausting, physically taxing, faith-stretching journey. Lyme disease and PTSD have similar symptoms; this means she's bombarded constantly by a succession of debilitating waves. She's had multiple ER visits, along with an ambulance ride, thinking she was having heart issues. But it was only severe anxiety, a result of PTSD. Mia and I had our own ER visits for the same reason.

Julia and I stand in the kitchen, holding one another tightly. She rubs my ponytail and gently pats the back of my head.

Lord, protect her! Heal her. Hold her. Come to her. Lead her. Guide her way. Keep her surrounded on every side. I'm trusting You, God; her heart and body are in Your hands.

"When you pass through the waters, I will be with you; and through the rivers, they shall not overwhelm you."

In trouble like this I need loyal friends—whether I've forsaken God or not. (Job 6:14 GNT)

After the unexpected cold snap, my friends continue entering into my pain and filling the voids in my life. They help carry me through this time of loneliness. I sit across the table from my friend Amy while we drink cappuccinos in a local coffee shop. She shares something with me that pulls me away on a quick silent walk with God. My heart melts in awe at His faithfulness to me; He shows me what the fellowship of suffering looks like.

Amy and I talk about life, our struggles, my fears, my heart, our journey, our hope, and our mutual belief that God is faithful. One hour into our conversation, she casually mentions a journal my sister Jerri gave her and a handful of other friends at a luncheon a couple of months after Michael died. Jerri had invited women who were instrumental in holding me up (physically and spiritually) and who had even run my household that first horrendous week, when getting out of bed, dressing for the day, and sitting in my kitchen was the most I could do during that stage of shock. Those days were, and still are, a blur to me.

Amy tells me she began using this journal as a prayer journal for my kids and me. She prays for us continually and records her prayers, adding notes about how God shows His answers through events in our lives. She says she looked through it recently and clearly sees how God is holding us in His hand, carrying us, and keeping us in that safe place. Looking at me across the table, she says, "He is not going to allow you to hide, because He has done great things in you and He will be glorified for it." As she speaks these words, I'm thinking, *Who am I to be blessed with such a fellowship of friends who would faithfully pray for my kids and me, listen to God for how to pray for us, and stay in it for the long haul with me?* I listen to her as my throat forces down a big lump and gratitude washes over me. I'm amazed by how God placed friends in my life ahead of time who practice such a deep level of fellowship with me, *the fellowship of suffering.*

In his book *What on Earth Am I Here For?*, Rick Warren explains that there are four levels of fellowship. He describes the fourth level this way: "The deepest, most intense is the fellowship of suffering, where we enter into each other's pain and grief and carry each other's burdens." A couple months after Michael died, I spoke with the wife of one of Michael's colleagues. She said people miss out on so much by not "going there" with those who are grieving. She told me it's such a precious time to share with those we love; we learn much through it. Warren continues, "It is in the times of deep crisis, grief, and doubt that we need each other most. When circumstances crush us to the point that our faith falters, that's when we need believing friends the most. We need a small group of friends to have faith in God for us and to pull us through." I'm abundantly blessed with more than one friend who fits into the category of one who will "enter into each other's pain and grief and carry each other's burdens."

There is nothing that will test our friendships more, or cause our relationships to build and mature with more strength, than death and grieving. I'm honored and privileged to have the remaining incredibly strong friendships. They continue to build, mature, strengthen, and deepen. The friends who remain constant are those who continue coming toward me. They don't simply say, "You know I am here if you need me. Just give me a call." It doesn't work this way. These friends take the initiative and call to check in with me on a continual basis. They offer their ears to listen, a shoulder for me to cry on, and their time when I need companionship. This is what the fellowship of suffering looks like.

I have spoken to countless people who have suffered loss, and they all contend that calling someone when they had a need wasn't something they did, even though the invitation was put out there by well-meaning friends. During this stage of grieving, it requires too much strength and effort to reach out this way. Not only is it too much effort, we don't always know our needs. We cannot think or take our emotions very far beyond our self-imposed grief boundaries. Friends are welcome to enter into these boundaries, but it isn't often we leave our boundaries, looking for a listening ear or help in any way. We need the support to come *to* us.

I'm thankful and honor my friends who come and have the courage to enter into the grief boundaries surrounding me. They give and give without expecting anything in return. I have had one-sided friendships with these friends since Michael died. I've needed much without having anything to give. I honestly have a difficult time even caring about the daily grind in anybody's life outside of my boundaries. Nothing but life itself and love matter to me right now. In my heart, I want to be more of a friend in return for them, but I can't physically do it. The ability is slowly emerging, which means my friends will continue residing with me, inside my boundaries, as they expand and broaden a little more each day.

CHAPTER 13

Behold, the Bridegroom!

When you realize you want to spend the rest of your
life with somebody, you want the rest of your life to
start as soon as possible.

—HARRY BURNS FROM *WHEN HARRY MET SALLY*

I FINALLY SWITCHED TO THE OTHER SIDE—sleeping on the other
side of the bed, that is.

It's a first for me. I did some research on what other people
have to say about switching sides of the bed after losing a loved
one. Many spoke of its difficulty, some tried it unsuccessfully
and went back to their same old side, while others very simply made the switch. I couldn't find any true insight on the
benefits of switching. The only helpful insight I found was
that it's easier to handle the night and sleep better if your *own*
side is empty instead of theirs. I found a much bigger meaning to switching sides, but first I had to examine why I hadn't
switched sides before now.

I felt safe on my side. His big, empty side was between the
door and me. The space gave me a sense of false security. I

was essentially hiding, emotionally and physically. Physically because I stacked up all of the extra pillows on his side, which made me feel as if I had a barrier. It also kept the bed from looking empty as I gazed in that direction in the dark. The long stack of pillows brought me added warmth, which is comforting when you're used to the extra body heat that comes from sharing the bed with someone. I had my own little safe haven on my side and in the corner. With my enormous stack of books on my nightstand, it was almost like being in a different room if I stayed tightly on my side. Switching sides for the purpose of sleeping well was not motivating, because it's been much better since we moved to New York, and if it ain't broke…

I didn't go to bed one night and suddenly switch sides. No, I eased my way over. I spent a week sleeping in the middle of the bed—I slept great. Small step, big victory. I found I slowly migrated to one side or the other and felt freedom and ownership of the newfound space. When putting my reading book on the nightstand or getting a drink of water became a problem (because sleeping in the middle of a king-sized bed creates much space between you and the nightstand), I decided to take the plunge and go completely to his side. The first night, even before I fell asleep, I felt as if I'd conquered scaling a wall; it felt like taking the deep breath of victory while enjoying the beautiful view from the top.

The feelings produced by switching sides are similar to what it must feel like to actually climb a mountain like Annapurna: empowered, strong, in control, courageous, and confident. The bed feels completely mine. It's like stepping into a role of new leadership. I'm discovering new parts of myself. I realize I *am* a risk taker. I am *not* afraid of new and different situations. I *can* walk into the unknown without fear holding me back. I am *much* more spontaneous than I've ever given myself credit for. I like the clear mind and clear thinking that come from less clutter in one's life—physical, mental, and emotional clutter. His nightstand was empty of books and sparsely decorated, which I like, whereas mine was full of books with just enough room for a coffee cup or a glass of water; I had been hiding with my books in my little corner. I'm no longer hiding behind anything in life.

I've been hiding by not answering my phone, not returning calls, not reading e-mails, not replying to e-mails, not reading Facebook private messages, not wanting to smile and be myself in pictures, hiding behind sunglasses, and not making eye contact. I'm tired of hiding. Switching sides of the bed and seeing my little corner where I'd been hiding since Michael died gives me a fresh new perspective.

The first morning after I switch sides, Julia walks into my bedroom and twists up her brow and says, "Why are you sleeping over here?" I reply, "I've been wanting to try it out," then add, "Besides, it's supposed to be healthy." She giggles and says, "And how can *that* be healthy?" She's thinking I mean healthy like drinking green drinks and taking vitamin C every day are healthy. I explain to her that it's emotional and mental health, a good and necessary step for someone who's lost a spouse. I see the light go on in her mind.

While in the process of switching sides, I simultaneously buy new organic sheets, Italian hotel bedding, new pillows, and a new headboard. Everything is white, except the headboard, which is covered in natural linen. It's all pure, new, fresh, simple, uncomplicated, and beautiful. I feel like I'm indulging myself every night as I climb into my new bed—another step toward a new life. I look at the bed now when I walk into my room, and instead of my gaze skipping over his side and focusing on my side tucked in the corner, I "see" the whole bed and I think, *What a beautiful bed!*

Switching sides is such a seemingly simple act but with huge implications. I feel as if I've cast off my ankle weights. I move onward a little bit farther down this new, unchartered road. This small step of moving on also helps keep my eyes looking to the future, because I *do* have a future and God has good things planned—in this I am confident. Switching sides shows I *am* keeping my heart purpose-minded in the here and now.

Why did I wait so long? It was a season. It's a new season now—on the other side.

Some friends lend me the use of their condominium on the beach as a retreat. I sit on the balcony, staring at the water. I listen to the waves as they near the shore. The breeze gently blows on my face on this quiet morning. I close my eyes; the sun warms my face. The water is tranquil, waves lapping in with the gentle pull of the tide, like a calm morning after a night storm. God's peace is palpable. He speaks to me: "The Midnight Hour is over. You have emerged on the other side." The sun is shining—a new day has dawned. The reverberations of the wave train after my tsunami are imperceptible. The seascape of grief has finally settled into a calm morning.

I anticipated a new level of healing this week because my communication with God is completely restored, the silencing fog lifted. I felt as if there had been a muzzle on my mouth, like I'd gone mute while in His presence. That's the terrible byproduct of grief: it strikes us dumb and isolates us, even in our faith. Now, at last, God and I are talking again, I to Him, and He to me.

The journey through the Midnight Hour made me feel as if I were far away from home. Now I'm back, and it's good to be home. It felt like watching the sunrise on a beautiful morning. First the glow, then the colors, and then, suddenly, the sun appears. It reminds me of the parable of the ten virgins where Jesus says in Matthew 25:6, "But at midnight there was a shout, 'Behold, the bridegroom! Come out to meet *him*'" (NASB). I came out to meet him.

In *My Utmost for His Highest*, Oswald Chambers says silence with God is the first sign of intimacy:

Has God trusted you with a silence—a silence that is big with meaning? God's silences are His answers...God will give you the blessings you ask if you will not go any further without them; but His silence is the sign that He is bringing you into a marvelous understanding of Himself. Are you mourning before God because you have not had an audible response? You will find that God has trusted you in the most intimate way possible, with an absolute silence, not of despair, but of pleasure, because He saw that you could stand a bigger revelation. If God has given you a silence, praise Him, He is bringing you into the great run of His purposes.

God's silences are His answers. His silence can mean *Wait, Don't move, Not yet, Sit with me,* or *Rest here awhile.* He doesn't need words to guide us. I imagine I'm walking on a path right behind Him. He perceives something ahead. He reaches back, touches my arm, and then holds His finger to His mouth, signaling not to speak. We both listen intently. He decides it's best to stop and rest, to set up camp here for a bit until He feels it's safe and I'm strong enough for the journey that still lies ahead of us. But we must remain silent in the darkness of the woods. I trust Him as "He is bringing me into the great run of His purposes."

God is putting my heart and my life back together, back together to fulfill His purposes. I'm seeing a few parts of the puzzle settle into place. Before Michael died, the puzzle felt as if it was closing in on the full picture but then was dumped out all over again. Of course God isn't starting with the edge pieces, which is the way I like to put puzzles together. It establishes boundaries, lets me know where I am going with it. The pieces God chose to put together first are somewhere in the middle of the puzzle. I can't picture where He'll place them yet within the picture, but the process of building, mending, and putting back together has begun.

I continue experiencing some loneliness. My connection to my Heavenly Father helps. I draw even closer as I depend on Him to fill the loneliness with His presence, comfort, and peace. Sometimes I feel it, sometimes I don't. My wanderings alone with God stretched my faith. I know, no matter how I feel, that He is there.

We are talking *because* it's time to put things back together. Seasons end. Seasons begin. He knows it's time to move forward again on our journey. To say that progress wasn't made during the silent stage would be far from the truth. He held my hand and silently showed me things. My silent time with God gave me a perspective I couldn't have seen had we been talking all of the time. He gave me glimpses of the whole picture, snapshots so I could know His unfailing love had *not* vanished. He allowed me to dream. He's showing me how His plan is falling into place.

He is creating a beautiful picture again.

God also showed me how to pray. I asked Him to write my prayers. Our needs for continued healing and restored lives were so great that I didn't even know how to pray. So I asked for His prayers for me. His answer: "Pray the resurrection power of Christ over your household."

Why hadn't I thought of that before?

Of course I should pray the resurrection power over the kids and me; it covers everything! We needed the stone to roll away so we could emerge among the living again. I wanted to be fully alive again. I wanted my children to be fully alive again. I wanted God to resurrect every part of us. My prayers began to pour out of my heart as if a floodgate had lifted. Our needs for life were great and had built up, but it was time to release the dam.

Lord, I pray the resurrection power of Christ over me. Resurrect my heart from the dead. Resurrect my hope for the future. Resurrect my joy, my boldness. Resurrect my dreams. Resurrect my life from the ashes. Resurrect my creativity and my gifts that I have lost the desire to use. Resurrect my desires, my purpose.

Resurrect my dance. Restore me; restore my family, with the same power that restored Christ after his death on the cross.

I personalized this prayer for each of my children. It became my daily prayer as I cried out to God to lift our lives out from the ashes that remained from my Michael's death. We needed a complete, glorified resurrection, just as Jesus did. After three months of this prayer, the resurrection power lifted the gate just as it rolled away the stone from the tomb for Jesus. It felt like the sun opening up on an overcast afternoon with its warmth enveloping every inch of my body.

My thoughts are now consumed with the idea of awakened souls and resurrected desires, and then I open my e-mail to see this daily reading from John Eldredge's book, coauthored by the late Brent Curtis, *The Sacred Romance*:

Desire often feels like an enemy, because it wakes longings that cannot be fulfilled in the moment... Spring awakens a desire for the summer that is not yet. Awakened souls are often disappointed, but our disappointment can lead us onward, actually increasing our desire and lifting it toward its true passion.

Everything has been resurrected; I feel it. God heard me. He responded. He brought me back among the living, but now what?

I feel like a racehorse in the gate before a big race, full of energy, strength, desire, and purpose, but still held back by the gate. I see the track before me, but it's not yet the moment. My resurrected desires feel ready, and I'm recognizing purpose again. "Desire often feels like an enemy, because it wakes longings that cannot be fulfilled in the moment." I fight frustration with my resurrected desire for life, as if it is the enemy. It's not the moment, and yet I feel so ready.

It reminds me of a quote from one of my favorite movies, *When Harry Met Sally.* Harry says to Sally near the end of the movie, "When you realize you want to spend the rest of your life with somebody, you want the rest of your life to start as soon as possible." I translate this as: When you realize *how* you want to spend the rest of your life, you want the rest of your life to start as soon as possible.

What encourages me is knowing that God wouldn't resurrect all of these things if it were not close to the time to open the gate. The Message version of Romans 8:15–21 helps me understand this quandary:

This resurrection life you received from God is not a timid, grave-tending life. It's adventurously expectant, greeting God with a childlike "What's next, Papa?" God's Spirit touches our spirits and confirms who we really are. We know who he is, and we know who we are: Father and children. And we know we are going to get what's coming to us—an unbelievable inheritance!... That's why I don't think there's any comparison between the present hard times and the coming good times. The created world itself can hardly wait for what's coming next. Everything in creation is being more or less held back. God reins it in until both creation and all the creatures are ready to be released at the same moment into the glorious times ahead. Meanwhile, the joyful anticipation deepens.

After several years in the tomb, I feel adventurously expectant, asking God, "What's next, Papa?" Meanwhile, the joyful anticipation deepens as I wait for release to the glorious times ahead. The long winter is finally over. Spring has returned! My life is restored as perennials come back to life and beauty after a season of dormancy. It's renewed like the new growth on a rosebush after a hard prune, a prune that cuts off every limb of the lovely plant, but then, somehow, miraculously, the plant comes back more beautiful and stronger than before.

With desire for life and purpose awakening from their deep slumber, other areas begin awakening. The dance in me begins stirring. I once danced through life in total abandonment. How long had it been since I'd danced like that? I've done it before, more times than I can count. Most every day of my life. If there was a song, there was a dance. My dancing grew from a hobby to a twenty-year profession. But I buried my dance long ago, buried my dancing to music and my dancing with life. I buried it even before Michael died. It sank deeper into the grave beside him after his death. I thought, *How can I ever dance again?*

It's time. Time to stir up the dancer—and the dance—in me.

I find irony in Ecclesiastes 3. Here is the famous listing of a time for everything: "a time to be born and a time to die, a time to plant and a time to uproot, a time to kill and a time to heal, a time to tear down and a time to build, a time to weep and a time to laugh, a time to mourn and a time to dance"(NIV).

How is it that dancing follows mourning? These two are a pair? Really? It's hard to swallow this one, but it must be so, just as the others hold true. As naturally as dying eventually follows birth, and building naturally follows tearing down, dancing should naturally follow on the tails of mourning. Joyful abandonment. Freedom to enjoy life again. The weight of grief lifted. Moving creatively and gracefully through life. Expressions of thankfulness for life itself.

It's time to resurrect the dance.

I've watched the resurrection slowly take place in each of us, in small steps and in different areas. In my life, the resurrection of hope and desire led to a natural resurrection in other areas. Because desire is alive again, I choose to reach down to Dance and pull her out of the ashes. I whisper to her, "Shall we dance?"

A time to mourn and a time to dance.

In 2 Samuel 6:14, scantily clad King David danced before the Lord with all of his might. In reference to this Scripture, Joshua Dubois writes in his book, *The President's Devotional*, "He danced because the Lord had been good. He danced because despite unspeakable trials, he was still alive. He danced because it gave glory and honor to the God who had formed him in his mother's womb. He danced because the weight of sin had been lifted off of him. He danced, and danced, and then danced some more, with all that he had."

Dancing in total abandonment is not limited only to dancing physically. The way I live my life, approach it, experience it, can also be a dance of abandonment executed with passionate, uninhibited zeal. Living free, without a care of what others may think. Living life from the heart. Moving seamlessly in step with my dreams, my purpose. Exuberant living. As a body moves to the rhythm of the music, bringing a song to life, so my life can move and glide along with life itself, its rhythm, its pulse, while bringing subtle inspiration to those watching the dance.

Proverbs 16:3 has been a foundational building block for me for decades, especially meaningful since Michael died. A verse I memorized long ago, scribbled on notes and woven into my daily prayers for as long as I can remember:

Commit your works to the LORD,
and your thoughts will be established. (NKJV)

I love the words "your thoughts will be established." I've prayed this Scripture for clear thinking in all I do. Clear thinking then produces successful work, plans, and actions. Michael's death taught me a new angle. I never connected this verse directly to purpose until I read this footnote to Proverbs 16:3 in my *Spirit Filled Bible, New King James Version*, even though I read it countless times before. An epiphany takes place:

If one turns over to the Lord what he plans to do, his life purposes will come to fruition.

His life purposes *will* come to fruition. *My purpose will come.* God's word pierces straight to my heart.

At lunch today I feel my purpose and passion burning a

slow dance together in a single movement for the first time. I'm with a friend, a rare outing for me. Seated by a window in one of my favorite restaurants, we discuss a range of topics. She mentions her concern for her father-in-law. He's changed jobs countless times throughout his life and now, in his mid-sixties, is a salesman in a local store. She talks as if she longs for him to find that "something" he's yet to discover in life. Listening to her speak, I feel *his* disappointment with life. It settles on me like a burden. I ask her, "Has he not ever found his passion in life?" She says no.

I divert my gaze out the window; my eyes spill over with tears. The lump is in my throat, but it's for someone else's pain now. A moment passes. I turn back and soberly say, "What a tragedy—living your whole life without ever discovering or living out your passion." Life's too short *not* to follow our passions. To not ever know what makes your adrenaline flow? What brings you joy? What brings you life and energy? What a mundane life it would be without passion.

I now hurt for people who haven't discovered their passions, their unique glory and role in this life. I hurt for those who have buried passion or lost it. I hurt for all of the couples who never discover their passion in life together.

About a year before Michael died, I felt as if I'd lost my passion for life, a very low place to be. We were out for dinner when he recognized that my recently dampened spirit was not changing. He asked me, "Babe, what are you passionate about?" I admitted that I had slowly, over several months, lost my way. I couldn't see or feel my passion anymore. He'd been busy planning his business merger, and I was consumed with taking care of our foster child, fighting for his rights against the bureaucracy, and I had recently been informed that he would not be up for adoption. My passion led to a broken heart, the downside to living with passion. A broken heart from following your passion hurts more than where there is no passion at stake.

People say it's better to have loved and lost than never to have loved at all. I say it's also better to live with passion and experience the disappointments and heartache than to go through life without ever discovering your passion—or, even worse, to discover it but then not have the courage to live in it and pursue it. It's the risk we take with passion, but living our passion is worth every bit of the risk. Being a foster parent was a risk, but we were passionate about caring for a child in need of love, security, and family. And because we were passionate, a child's life was protected.

My passion, my desire to chase after life, never fully recovered before Michael died. Then it bottomed out. It was neutral and numb. I felt as if I'd come to a crossroads. My passion and purpose were taking me into unknown territory, and I couldn't see any light ahead in either direction. Then Michael suddenly died. Passion and desire went into a long season of dormancy. Like a caterpillar changes into a beautiful butterfly, I knew my passion would emerge, more glorious than before. Even in the middle of the darkest days of the Midnight Hour, I knew it would emerge somewhere along the road.

New passions began to take over. My passion to pull through the Midnight Hour and cover my children with all of my love and support motivated me daily. That passion remains. I'm also passionate about living sold out to God. Not in a religious, dutiful way, but in an adventurous relationship with Him, following every twist and turn in the road He lays before me. I want to live a deliberate life and live it well, with passion leading the way. Walking silently with God through the Midnight Hour brought about a paradigm shift in my entire outlook on life and living. I feel completely free with Him again. And so we dance together.

My proverb, my mantra, propels me continually. It gives me focus each day on the unique blend of passion and purpose God placed in me: "Let your eyes look straight ahead and your eyelids look right before you. Ponder the path of your feet, and let all your ways be established." I want every step to count for God. I don't want to rush through life. I want to live my life in the moment and hear God all along the way. I want to see people through the lens of the love of Jesus, through His eyes of compassion. I want to love people through their pain, their trials, or their faults. I choose to embrace the ministry God created through my blog. I'm passionate to help others get beyond their trials and discover *their* passion for life.

Passion is married to purpose. Once passion is fueled, purpose falls into place. I feel the pieces in my life falling into place. I take up my refueled passion, my redirected purpose, and the new map God gave me. I'm embarking on a new journey with Him. I see the path before me with more clarity now; I trust the way He's crafted these things together.

CHAPTER 14

More Than a Conqueror

In all these things, we are more than conquerors
through him who loved us.

—ROMANS 8:37 (NIV)

TODAY BEGINS THE LAST YEAR of my forties. My fifth birthday without Michael. Even with the passage of time, today feels vague, lonely, and contemplative. Maybe it's because Nanette spent my last two birthdays in New York with me and today there are no houseguests. Maybe it's because so much has changed since my first birthday without him. Maybe it's because the house is so quiet. Birthdays were once mornings of energy, family time, and celebration of life over a big breakfast, with the kids as excited as if it were their own birthdays. Today Mia is out of town, Michael Anthony is still sleeping, and Julia is quietly and happily buzzing around in the kitchen. She brings me coffee in bed, along with an endearing letter she's written to me. She comes back with warm waffles and a gift. I sit alone in my quiet bedroom while looking out the sliding glass doors. I spot a large doe staring back at me. She slowly turns and walks across our property through the melting snow.

Yes, today is different. Each birthday is more and more different. But that's life. We grow, we change, life changes, kids leave the nest, and the more we move forward, the more we also leave behind. I'm thankful that the more I move forward, the more darkness and pain I leave behind. I'm thankful that I draw nearer to God with each passing day. I'm thankful for the friends God placed in my life along the journey—at the exact time and in the exact place I needed them.

I choose to be happy today, to love my life in spite of the trials, to love my God in spite of the trials—to love them more *because* of the trials. If a healed heart truly is more glorious than a heart that's never been wounded, then today will be glorious. My life will be glorious.

When Adam and Eve chose to eat the forbidden fruit in the Garden of Eden, their eyes suddenly opened to their nakedness, and they were instantly ashamed. They were "in all their glory," but their sin made them ashamed of their glory, the glory God created them to carry as image bearers of Him. They foolishly thought they could hide their glory from Him.

Strong's Concordance defines *glory* as "the unspoken manifestation of God, splendor, honor, renown, what evokes good opinion, i.e. that something has inherent, intrinsic worth, brightness—as of the moon, sun and stars, magnificence, dignity, excellence, grace, a thing belonging to God or Christ, a most glorious condition."

And we try to hide this?

I don't want to hide my glory. I read in Isaiah 61:3, "GOD sent me to...rename them [the captives] 'Oaks of Righteousness' planted by GOD to display his glory" (MSG). I want to display His glory, His magnificence, dignity, excellence, a glorious condition.

I was created, we were all created, to live and be free with our glory unleashed, but we're crippled with fear of our own glory. It's as bad as being afraid of our own shadow. Those we remember most in our lives or through history are typically those who lived their lives unleashed and exposed, fearless to reveal their glory. They left a legacy because they lived, loved, talked, and related to others "in all their glory."

Why is this so hard? Why push down the unique way I carry the image of God? In his book *Waking the Dead*, John Eldredge says it this way: "God endowed you with a glory when he created you, a glory so deep and mythic that all creation pales in comparison. A glory unique to you, just as your fingerprints are unique to you, just as the way you laugh is unique to you. Somewhere down deep inside we've been looking for that glory ever since." I don't want to cover up my glory; instead, I want to uncover it like a hidden treasure. What would be wrong with someone saying, "Yep, there's Jené in all her glory!"? Shouldn't that be a good thing?

And yet, we play it safe.

Did Jesus play it safe and keep his glory under wraps? He lived with his glory completely unleashed. Was King David mediocre in the way he worshipped God? I think dancing naked before God qualifies as living unleashed. I will no longer be lulled into believing that it's best to play it safe and hold back to a place of mediocrity. Living unleashed is a vulnerable place, but this isn't a good enough reason to justify not living in all my glory.

I think of a dog on a leash. He's restricted. The leash tells him how far he can go. What happens when a dog is released from his leash? He runs with joy and freedom, his true personality immediately exposed. He's in all his glory! Ironically, we hold our own leash. We need freedom. We need to release the leash. I need to release my leash. Unleash to live and walk fully in my glory. Unleash to be the free, beautiful, unique creation God intended me to be. God's love is unleashed. His glory is unleashed. I'm made in His image, so doesn't it only make sense that I live unleashed in my glory?

I choose unleashed living, the whole, complete, unashamed, glorious me. I choose what makes my heart feel glorious. I choose to cast off my afflictions. I choose to see only good in my future. I choose living in the present and looking to the future. I choose courage. I choose hope. I choose to fight the good fight. I choose the happy heart—the glad heart, the cheerful heart. If I can have this kind of heart each day, in spite of and regardless of my circumstances, the Scripture promises I'll have a continual feast, according to Proverbs 15:15. I'll have life with an unusual and abundant amount of enjoyment. Why would I *not* choose a continual feast in my life?

Life is a choice. How I'm going to live it each day is *my* choice.

I choose to keep my eyes straight ahead, not even looking down where I am presently standing, but looking ahead. Simply seeing one or two steps ahead is all it takes to keep moving forward and see the potential life to be lived. There is a purpose to my past, my present, and my future, and God has a plan for how it's all working together for my good. I choose life with abundant enjoyment. I choose to trust in that plan and believe for the best.

I choose to believe God's words; I truly *am* more than a conqueror! I *am* breathing again without reminding myself. I *am* laughing more frequently. I *am* excited about each new day, and I *am* looking to the future with heightened expectancy of something good. The sick feelings in the pit of my stomach are gone. The weight on my chest is gone. Sleepless nights, well, sometimes they still occur. No more daily tears. The day has come and I barely recognized it, because I crept up on it with baby steps. I conquered one thing at a time.

There are more baby steps ahead, but thank God the dark valley is behind me. I've pressed into life, kept my eyes straight ahead with each step, and focused on my purpose. I look behind me to see the great distance I've traveled. I notice this distance most clearly in unlikely places.

Who knew Sting and Paul Simon could bring on a spiritual awakening right in the middle of Madison Square Garden? I stand on the floor level, listening to them from the eighth row. I'm engulfed with a realization: I've created a new life for myself—through God's grace and by His mercy.

I've been a Sting fan since college, when he was with the Police, and I grew up in the seventies listening to the classic "vinyl" by Simon & Garfunkel. Seeing the two of them onstage in Madison Square Garden is magical for me. Tears surface; I cleverly hide them. Not tears because of who is onstage, but tears of joy over my life, the life God and I have created together. Created with the courage and strength He gave me, and my willingness to move forward with life. It's an awesome moment.

I've struggled with doing things that make me happy, holding back because I believe my happiness isn't important. But now I choose happiness. While Sting croons the lead of "Like a Bridge," I realize I am, at this moment, doing what I want to do simply because it's fun and it makes me happy. It confirms in my heart that I can, I did, and I do create my life. Even though I've been creating life since Michael died, I haven't felt I had the right to create life in *all* areas of my life. I will no longer be afraid to go after my dreams and be the whole person God created in me—unleashed. This doesn't just happen; it takes an intentional decision to move forward.

"Good things come to those who wait" is an old proverb, a slogan made popular by a Guinness advertising campaign. Good things don't always come to those who wait; sometimes the best things come to those who *do*, or make it happen—like creating life. I can't simply dream about my goals and desires. I must move toward them. With the music filling the arena, I recognize that I've moved toward a new life with intention. As with everything else, it was one step at a time, making it difficult to recognize how far I'd come into my newly created life—until now, as I hear Sting sing it:

Your time has come to shine
All your dreams are on their way
See how they shine

I feel I'm in a worship service. I want to raise my hands and praise God—He's been my bridge. He's bridged my life from pain and grief over to joy and dancing. He's bridged me from death and darkness over to new life and light. I'm in awe. I feel God confirm, "I was your bridge. We did it! You are here. You are alive and well! You are living! This is the other side. A new life has been created for you. A life for you to enjoy. A life to bring you happiness. I carried you over the bridge. What is behind you is behind you. What lies ahead of you is all new, a newly created life."

Today my newly created life shines in another unexpected area. It's Michael Anthony's sixteenth birthday—a milestone, and not just for him.

As I wrap his presents, an onslaught of emotions washes over me. I'm reminded again of the mystery and reality of one shall become two, one person filling the needs that before took two people to do successfully. The transition remains miraculous. The hardest part of being a female single parent is discerning the needs of a son without input from a man. It's an overwhelming responsibility. I shared this with my friend Barri yesterday at the gym. She said she sees me as both mother and father, transferring seamlessly between both roles automatically. She said she's noticed it became instinctive, as if I'm operating on autopilot. Some days it truly does feel like I'm on autopilot, while other days, like today, I feel as if I have nothing to offer this young man.

I think back to that moment on my bed with the kids when I asked them to be patient with me. I apologized in advance for failing. I told them there would be times I'd fail as a parent—I'd miss it. Today I feel more vulnerable as a parent than ever. I've conquered many obstacles, but parenting alone remains one of the hardest parts of this new life. My mind swims in these thoughts as I wrap Michael Anthony's presents.

While attending one of the Wild at Heart Boot Camps in Colorado given by Ransomed Heart Ministries, Michael purchased a William Wallace replica sword. He intended to give it to Michael Anthony at the perfect time to signify his crossing over from boyhood to manhood. He was ten years old when his father bought the sword. It's remained in the box until this moment, when I am wrapping presents for his sixteenth birthday.

I knew this birthday would be the perfect time to present the sword. Anticipating this, I had John Eldredge autograph a copy of his book *Wild at Heart* for him when I had the opportunity to meet him last fall. He wrote, "Happy 16th Birthday! You are this young man!" Michael Anthony is about to receive both of these gifts representing his masculine journey and the bridge from boyhood to manhood—the moment overwhelms me. I feel completely unqualified as a parent for him.

I'm overwhelmed that he has become a young man without his father, overwhelmed that I have raised a boy to become a mighty man of God, overwhelmed that I have encouraged him to be the man God created him to be. This precious young boy, who was twelve when his dad died and a whole foot shorter than he is now, has shown courage I didn't know was possible. He *is* doing it without his father. I'm overwhelmed at how he and I have navigated this together. I'm overwhelmed with sadness that he won't get to share his manhood with his father, but then I'm overwhelmed with pride at his hope for the future.

I delicately pull the sword out of the box, then slowly remove the bubble wrap that has protected it all these years. The air in the room feels heavy. Breathing is difficult. The blade glistens in the afternoon light coming through the blinds. The moment feels almost magical. I notice an inscription on the blade: WILD AT HEART. At this moment, the gravity of the gift weighs on my heart.

I stand to my feet. My eyes gaze over the hilt that is partially encased in leather, examining the extremely long blade. I grab the hilt with both hands, extending the sword out in front of me. I feel this moment empowering me to empower Michael Anthony to chase after his journey into manhood, to chase after his masculine spirit, which God placed in him, with every bit of courage and strength that is in him.

Then feelings of inadequacy set into my thoughts again: *What words do I have that I can say to him as he receives the gift? What can I, as a woman, say that would speak to his manhood and encourage him in the way of God? To encourage him to keep his heart wild for God and live with all of his glory unleashed?* I fight despair that there isn't a man who can speak into his life.

I collapse on the couch with the sword in my lap and cry like I haven't cried in years. As I cry out all the tears, a wave of courage washes over me. I take a deep breath; strength and empowerment fill me. I realize this is a journey for my son and me to do alone. I embrace the journey. God's grace carried me to this day and will continue to do so. *One became two.*

I feel commissioned to affirm him with the same words John Eldredge wrote in the book: "You are this man!" This man God created you to be. You are this man who has a purpose uniquely designed for you alone. You are this man we prayed since birth you'd become. You are this man—a mighty warrior. You are this man—valiant, strong, and masculine in heart. You are this man that your father saw in you. You are this man, wild at heart, just as God wants you to be.

I'm conquering one thing at a time—and this one is monumental.

This is not the end of the story. As with a fairy-tale ending, it's actually only the beginning. A new beginning. A beautiful beginning. Instead of reading "The End" on the last page, it says "Good night, I love you"—Michael's last words to me. And now I say good night to the days I loved with him by my side. Good night to that season of my life. Good night to the purposes God accomplished in me, in us, during those days. I say good night to Michael. I loved him and I loved him well.

Saying good night at the close of a day simply means a new day is coming; it's expected. I am expectant. The sun *will* rise again. My story continues with each new sunrise. With God, in this moment, I am more than a conqueror.

A new day has dawned.

But the path of the just *is* like the shining sun,
that shines ever brighter unto the perfect day.
(Proverbs 4:18 NKJV)

Good night, I love you.

Acknowledgments

I think of life like a river. A river knows where to go. My life knows where to go, and it's taking me there—and the current carries me outside the box. It knows what I need. The children and I are moving along together, as we have to, but in fundamental ways, alone—alone because every grieving person must grapple for guidance for his or her own journey through deep waters, trusting the river.

—*GOOD NIGHT, I LOVE YOU*

My travels with this book felt like a ride down a long, twisting river. The current carried us, the manuscript and me. We experienced rushing waters, floated serenely downriver at times, and were even caught in shallow waters every now and then. But just as a river knows, the manuscript knew where to go. It knew whom we needed along the way and took us there. God watched over the river and over us, reaching down to guide us gently in the direction He wanted us to go—and so I trusted Him as we floated down the river.

I am thankful for the river guides God placed along the banks. He used them to teach us and help move us to the next bend in the river. Sometimes they walked beside us, encouraging us to continue downriver. Sometimes they led, because they were familiar with the path; they knew the perfect guide to help us navigate the next part of the river. At other times they allowed us to lead, using the manuscript as the light that went before us.

⌒ ⌒

I want to acknowledge my experienced river guides:

Margot Schupf, my literary agent who found us sitting on the banks, the guide who placed my manuscript and me in the river and pushed us downstream. Thank you, Margot, for listening to me that day in the SoHo House as I shared my story with you. Thank you for believing there was a story inside me that the world needed to hear. And for believing I was capable to tell it. I am forever grateful for you as my initial guide.

Jane von Mehren, my literary agent who took the guiding torch from Margot. What steady peace and patience you exhibited as you stuck with me throughout the duration of the river ride. Your skills for gathering the proposal were exactly what we needed to complete the journey. You held my hand throughout the process, let it go when necessary, coached me, encouraged me, believed in me, pushed me. We did it, Jane. Thank you.

Joey Paul, my editor, the guide who spotted us on the river and believed we had what was necessary to make it to the end. He launched us out into the open waters. Joey, thank you for going out on a limb to guide us. You took a chance on this first-time author from Mississippi. Thank you for your confidence in us, your kindness toward us, and your gentleness with us— as we were still quite fragile from previous raging waters when we met. God used you in this crucial part of the journey.

Jacob Epstein, my fellow traveling writer and guide. When I told you about my story as our paths crossed on the river, you said, "I wish I'd had a book like that to read when my mother died." Thanks in part to you, you now have that book. Thank you for teaching me the power of structure and the art of moving sentences. Your input was invaluable.

Roger Rosenblatt, my surprising guide who held some clues and unknowingly unlocked a door for me. Roger, your master class writing series at Stony Brook Southampton Writers Conference opened up my horizon and pushed my slowing boat a little farther downriver.

Hachette Book Group and FaithWords, my guides into the open waters. You believed my voice is relevant and needed. Thank you for the opportunity to sail the sea.

Bankside supporters, my special friends who walked along the banks throughout the journey. Some were with me when the story began, a few joined in as I embarked at push-off, while others were led by God to the banks once the open waters were in sight. You read my chapters as I shared, encouraged me to keep going even when I barely had the strength to hold on another day. You believed in me when I doubted. You told me I could make it to the sea. Thank you. You helped carry me.

Mia, Julia, and Michael Anthony Barranco, my sailors whose hearts helped guide me. Thank you for your love and your courage to follow me on this journey. I am honored and privileged to be your guide. I love you.